"It's critical that caregivers have the opportunity to share their stories and *Wounded Warrior Wounded Wife* covers everything from personal stories to practical and useful advice. There is often no acknowledgment for caregivers. Barbara gives a voice to many who have never been heard. Thank you Barbara for promoting health, wellness, and stress reduction among caregivers and ultimately preventing caregiver burnout."

—Sara Boz, PhD,
operationhomefront.net, www.heartsofvalor.org

"I applaud Barbara McNally for bringing greater attention and awareness to a subject that so many struggle with. Through the stories and inspiration in her book, *Wounded Warrior Wounded Wife*, we see the opportunity to find healing at the end of an often very dark tunnel."

—Dave Towe, Executive Director, Wave Academy,
www.waveacademy.org

"Very inspiring and encouraging—a must-read for those who are caregivers for our wounded warriors. Especially loved the story of Mai and Lanh!"

—Penny Lambright, Founder, Patriots & Paws
www.patriotsandpaws.org

"A captivating ride through tragedy, trauma, resiliency, and strength of our amazing military caregivers. Our stories are our heartbeat, the threads that bind us together now and through the generations. Barbara has allowed these amazing women an opportunity to not only share their stories, but also a chance to evaluate and rewrite when necessary. Stories of weakness have become stories of strength. Stories of hopelessness have shifted into stories of survival. Her passion and desire to matter are evident through her writing, her mission, and her actions. A must read."

—Dr. Jude Black LPC, NCC, CEO | Founder E-Therapy Café™
www.e-therapycafe.com

"Barbara McNally shines the spotlight on the 1.1 million Post-9/11 military and veteran caregivers who so often live in the shadows. The women featured in this book are unsung heroes, that face daily challenges, caring for their families that have been forever changed by the wars. Kudos to Ms.McNally for elevating the visibility of military and veteran caregivers everywhere."

—Lorie Van Tilburg, Executive Director,
Southern Caregiver Resource Center
www.caregivercenter.org

"Barbara McNally's *Wounded Warrior Wounded Wife* is a must read for wives attempting to understand and support their husbands as they struggle with reorienting their lives after suffering service related trauma. Over the years, within Project Healing Waters Fly Fishing, I have witnessed just how important it is for couples to understand each other in a totally different emotional and physical environment. Barbara's book should find a place in all homes where greater insight and help is needed for couples struggling to meet the challenges of a new order."

—Ed Nicholson, Capt, USN (RET) Founder and President,
Project Healing Waters Fly Fishing
www.projecthealingwaters.org

"*Wounded Warrior, Wounded Wife* is powerful and engaging, a much needed acknowledgement that family members are serving, too. Barbara McNally profoundly shares through their stories the extraordinary challenges they face. We must do more in providing support and resources to all members of military families, and especially for those who have had to shift their lives and become caretakers. I will be recommending this book as a must-read for all who work with military members!"

—Lynn Thomas, LCSW, Founder & CEO, EAGALA
(Equine Assisted Growth and Learning Association),
eagala.org

"*Wounded Warrior, Wounded Wife* shines a critical spotlight on the heroes behind the heroes: wives thrust into the role of inspiring caregivers to their returning wounded warriors. In telling their individual stories, Barbara McNally's words resonate with each of us, whether we are caregivers, family, friends, or anyone wanting to be inspired by how these amazing women each met adversity head-on, with courage and class."

—Marjorie Morrison, author of The Inside Battle and
founder of Psych Armor
http://www.psycharmor.org/gala-sponsorship

"Not only does Barbara McNally write with passion, but she also reminds all of us that while an individual person may go off to war, it is the entire family that truly serves. In *Wounded Warrior, Wounded Wife*, we are shown the raw emotions and struggles that Veterans and their families must face when the fighting stops but the battle rages on at home…"

—Dr. Rob Uniszkiewicz, author of *The Bucket List Chronicles*,
http://www.koehlerbooks.com/books-2/books/bucket-list-chronicles/

"In the closing years of America's longest war, Barbara exposes what many suspected but never voiced: Spousal Post Traumatic Stress. She brings to light in her work the fact that where there's a wounded warrior, there's a wounded lover. Her research interviewing hundreds of warriors' wives addresses the unasked question, what happens to the warrior's spouse after the battles are over? A must read for military family readiness groups and concerned citizens."

—Command Sergeant Major Dennis J. Woods,
author of *Black Flag Journals*, www.threattec.com/

"In *Wounded Warrior, Wounded Wife* Barbara McNally offers hope to the millions of wives struggling to cope with the unseen afflictions of wounded heroes returning from the Middle East. It is a must read for every woman struggling to rescue her husband from throes of his demons, including PTSD, sexual dysfunction, anger issues, depression, and others, each with the specter of suicide lurking in the shadows of his mind. McNally possesses a hard-earned encyclopedic knowledge of her subject, and compassion and understanding drip from her every word. Had I the power to award it, she would receive a silver star, at the very least!"

—Larry Rogers, MD, author of Sword and Scalpel: *A Doctor Looks Back at Vietnam* and *M. Gazi Yasargil: Father of Modern Neurosurgery*

"Wounded Warrior, Wounded Wife will open your heart and inspire you to be a part of veterans and their spouses' lives."

—Elise Anne Marie, author of *Toy Soldiers*
www.eliseannemarie.com

"Barbara McNally's *Wounded Warrior, Wounded Wife* grips your heart and won't let go. Through a series of factual sketches, McNally paints a much larger portrait, one of courage, commitment, and love in the face of tragedy. Although the warriors' injuries bear some similarity in cause and impact, the real story lies in the diversity of the effect on their wives and how they respond when thrust into the unfamiliar and demanding role of caregiver. The result is a master class on Post Traumatic Growth, the positive change experienced by people who face a major crisis in their life. Kudos to McNally for the support she provides the wives though her SPA (Support, Purpose and Appreciation) days and for sharing their stories with us."

—Ron McManus, Author of *The Drone Enigma*,
ron-mcmanus.com

"Wounded Warrior Wounded Wife provides the reader with a stark view of the trials our soldiers face when they return from war. Barbara McNally exposes the sometimes un-pleasantries of trying to return to normalcy when life has been changed by TBI, PTSD, or amputation. The stories she tells are woven from interviews with caregivers, spouses, and veterans just trying to cope with a life changed forever by war. The book is a poignant look at survival of family and love. A must-read for all Americans that support our freedom. Exceptionally written!"

—J.R. Sharp, CDR, USN (ret), author of Feeding the Enemy
www.jrsharpauthor.com

"As a wife of a three-time deployed veteran Marine the raw truth in this book was like looking into the lives of those closest to me for a five-year time frame. This book dealt with the good and the bad of PTS and most endearing of the well-written book was the HOPE provided. I can't begin to express how moved I was by this book. It was a real life look for anyone who hasn't lived the dark, depressing world of PTS... If you need hope for restoration in your battle as a caregiver of someone facing the demons of war or any other high stress job I would recommend you pick up a copy of this book. May God continue to bless this author and her good works."

—Martina Dewey, Educator

"Wounded Warrior, Wounded Wife provides much needed insight into the lives of our military heroes and their families. Through these stories we learn how we can begin to create a healing environment through caring, compassion, community support and love for one another."

—Susan Stone, CEO Sharp Coronado Hospital

"*Wounded Warrior Wounded Wife* shines a spotlight on the often unspoken side of wounds and healing throughout the ages. It shows the impact on those transformed from being a companion, lover and partner to suddenly becoming a full time caregiver as a result of tragedy. Barbara McNally's book is relevant to anyone facing this challenge of caring for someone they love who is unexpectedly wounded as a result of war, accident or illness. These individuals are a large and growing part of our population who deserve recognition. Barbara's book does just that and more."

—Farrell Gallagher, LCSW, MFT

Wounded Warrior, Wounded Wife
Not Just Surviving but Thriving

by Barbara K. McNally

Thank you J.T. McMillian for the cover and author photo image

An imperint of

köhlerbooks™

210 60th Street
Virginia Beach, VA 23451
800-435-4811
www.koehlerbooks.com

barbaramcnally.com

WOUNDED

WARRIOR

WOUNDED

WIFE

NOT JUST SURVIVING BUT THRIVING

BARBARA K. MCNALLY

VIRGINIA BEACH
CAPE CHARLES

I dedicate this book to the man on the bridge and his family. And to the courageous and generous-hearted women who shared intimate details about the effects of wartime and home-front battles on their veterans, their families, and themselves. Their stories will certainly inspire and encourage many, many others in need of support and understanding as they take their own healing journeys.

Invictus

Out of the night that covers me,
Black as the pit from pole to pole,
I thank whatever gods may be
For my unconquerable soul.

In the fell clutch of circumstance
I have not winced nor cried aloud.
Under the bludgeonings of chance
My head is bloody, but unbowed.

Beyond this place of wrath and tears
Looms but the Horror of the shade,
And yet the menace of the years
Finds, and shall find me, unafraid.

It matters not how strait the gate,
How charged with punishments the scroll,
I am the master of my fate:
I am the captain of my soul.

—William Henley, 1875

Contents

Appendices

FOREWORD

THROUGH THE STORIES she shares here, Barbara McNally helps us understand a topic that nobody wants to talk about. Nobody, that is, except for the millions of women who haven't had a voice.

For a long time now, one of our nation's darkest secrets has been about what happens to the wounded warrior and his wife after the tours and the battles are over. We acknowledge the financial cost of war, but not the emotional costs. Now, thanks to Barbara's research and her work interviewing hundreds of wounded warriors' wives, these women finally have a platform to share their stories. Each of the book's selected stories illustrates phases of the recovery process from the perspective of the wife. Barbara also looks to experts in medicine, counseling, and social work for the advice she weaves into each chapter, advice millions of American women can use to survive the aftermath of war and other challenges that life brings.

The stories you will read in this book reflect what our nation's military caregivers deal with on a daily basis. Whether it's helping a spouse through an emotional meltdown, tracking negative side effects of various pain medications, helping a spouse on and off the toilet, or advocating for better mental health care, these caregivers are doing what they do out of love, devotion, friendship, and sometimes because there simply is no one else to do it. They are saving our long-term health-care system billions of dollars.

According to a 2014 study by the RAND Corporation, *Hidden Heroes: America's Military Caregivers,* there are 5.5 million military caregivers in the United States. Of these, nearly 20 percent (1.1 million) are caring for someone who served in the military after the terrorist attacks of September 11, 2001. In comparing military caregivers with their civilian counterparts, the study found that caregivers helping veterans from earlier eras tend to resemble civilian caregivers in many ways; by contrast, post-9/11 military caregivers differ systematically from the other two groups. Post-9/11 military caregivers are more likely to be

- younger (more than 40 percent are between ages eighteen and thirty);
- caring for a younger individual with a mental health or substance use condition;
- nonwhite;
- veterans of military service themselves;
- employed;
- not connected to a support network.

All of these factors make it even more challenging and taxing to care for an injured loved one.

But these women caregivers are strong—military strong! Leading us through their stories, Barbara shines a light on their attitudes, their reflections, and their actions in meeting and healing the wounds war brings. We begin to heal only when we are willing to examine the forces that have wounded us. When we know the problem, we can move toward solutions. Barbara's book is not only for those women living through the experience of caregiving for wounded warriors, but also for those of us who want to understand and to be of help. *Wounded Warrior, Wounded Wife* provides a clear view of the true price of war.

Our organization is proud to be included in the list of resources for this book. Our hope is that more wives of wounded warriors will connect with us and with the other all-too-often overlooked services created for helping them in difficult times.

May the women who have shared their stories serve as inspiration to all of us, proving that devoted love heals.

Laura J. Bauer

National Program Director, Operation Family Caregiver
Rosalynn Carter Institute for Caregiving
www.operationfamilycaregiver.org

PREFACE

THROUGH MY WORK, both as a physical therapist and as founder of the Barbara McNally Foundation, I have had the privilege of spending time with the wives and caregivers of hundreds of wounded warriors. With little warning and almost no training, these women have learned to serve their families as full-time caregivers while their partners try to recover from broken bones, lost limbs, severe head injuries, and other unspeakable assaults on their bodies and beings.

Each woman has a compelling story about how her life has changed since her husband returned home and where that journey has taken her. Over the past eight years, I've heard those stories twice a year at SPA Day—named for Support, Purpose, and Appreciation—which I sponsor for wives and caregivers of wounded warriors. More than 300 women apply for SPA Day, but at this time I am only able to accommodate thirty attendees. Everyone gets a spa treatment in the morning, then we gather for lunch by the pool. During this mini-retreat, women share and connect with others who are experiencing parallel struggles. This sharing helps all of them build their coping skills and find useful resources. Women come to the Hotel del Coronado in Southern California from all over the United States, from as far away as Hawaii and Florida, for a weekend of much-needed restoration and rejuvenation.

The women—who might not know one another before SPA Day—quickly form bonds that few can fathom. They've all had similar life-altering experiences dealing with catastrophic challenges, both physical and emotional, and these shared experiences unite them in a kind of instant sisterhood. Although some start the spa sessions feeling guarded and a bit anxious, their warm natures and supportive spirits emerge as they open up to one another. They talk openly about broken marriages, ruined sex lives, and suicide attempts. They share the memories of violent confrontations, hurtful accusations, and the cold, silent stares of lovers made unrecognizable by posttraumatic stress. They share horrific hospital stories, awkward wheelchair anecdotes, and memories of deflecting uncomfortable looks from strangers.

For many women, SPA Day is the first time they've been away from their husbands, and the first day they've had to themselves in months or even years. After taking care of their spouses for so long, they've forgotten what it's like to pamper themselves. Most women don't come to SPA Day expecting to talk openly about their struggles, but almost all of them do so when they find themselves surrounded by nurturing, caring women who truly understand their circumstances. They recognize each other, because they are reflections of one another.

SPA Day is about so much more than manicures and massages. It's about healing. The women's willingness to share their stories transforms the day. Those who have been holding on to the notion that they can "be strong and do anything" suddenly let their masks slip. They share their concerns, their fears, and their worries about the future in the first safe space many of them have known since their vet's return.

Theirs are stories of triumph and joy as well as disappointment and heartbreak, stories that are too rarely told in the media or public forums. I became inspired to share them here because they need and deserve to be heard. By bringing these stories to light, I hope to make more people aware that the struggles veterans face become struggles for their wives and family members, too. These stories are a tribute to the women who perform the selfless acts of strength and devotion necessary to live through the damage and pain of a spouse's military service having been cut short by devastating injuries.

These caretakers are the silent strength behind our soldiers, the troops on our home soil. Where there's a wounded warrior, there's a wounded lover—there's no way around it—and this is a topic that should be part of our national conversation.

So the next time you encounter a family with a wounded warrior, look for the woman by his side, and you will find someone who can teach you more about life than you ever dreamed possible. Read their stories here and learn from these women. Some names and identifying circumstances have been changed to protect their privacy.

Through the Barbara McNally Foundation, proceeds from this book's sales will provide more comfort, community building, healing opportunities, and leadership workshops for these committed and overworked women. For more information about these efforts, please visit www.BarbaraMcNally.com.

Barbara McNally
Barbara McNally Foundation

INTRODUCTION

THE BRIDGE FROM HERE TO THERE

WHILE I WAS driving across the Coronado Bridge, I saw a man jump to his death.

It was a beautiful May afternoon in San Diego, at around one-thirty. As I drove onto the bridge, I began releasing my morning's stress and started thinking about the things I would do when I got home. Admiring the boats in the bay, I started daydreaming about changing out of my tracksuit and into my tankini for a relaxing swim.

Suddenly, the car in front of me came to an abrupt halt. The driver-side door opened and a good-looking, well-dressed man in his late twenties got out. He was physically fit and had the grace of an athlete. He turned and faced me. I noticed that he had gorgeous brown hair. His brown eyes looked straight into mine. For whatever reason, I didn't feel alarmed or upset, even though what he was doing was decidedly out of the ordinary. He was calm and moved without hesitation, so I didn't think that either he or I were in any kind of danger. I assumed that his car had stalled or broken down and he was going to fix it. He certainly looked capable of it.

My curiosity changed into surprise and then to stomach-turning horror when he quickly moved to the edge of the lane, stepped over the knee-high barrier, and fell backward off the bridge.

No hesitation. No ambivalence. He was there one moment, and the next he was gone.

I fumbled for my phone and dialed 911, but it was already too late. There was nothing to do but wait for the police to come.

I later learned that he was a veteran. He went over the side as if it were a military maneuver, which he might have imagined it was: his last mission.

With a little digging, I learned that the man had lost his right arm from an improvised explosive device (IED) while deployed overseas. This detail surprised me, because I hadn't noticed it when he got out of his car that day on the bridge. I just noticed his face, his hair, his humanity. I also learned he left behind a wife and two small children. My work as a physical therapist has connected me with many other men and women who have returned from combat injured, just as he had. According to the U.S. Department of Veterans Affairs (VA), recent veterans are at a significantly higher risk of suicide than the general population. A study of veterans who served during the Iraq and Afghanistan wars found that warriors returning from deployment were 41 to 61 percent more likely to commit suicide compared to their civilian peers. These are some sobering numbers.

While it's understandable that military personnel would have limited access to support while they're deployed, it's obvious that they need it once they return to civilian life. The man who jumped off the bridge wasn't one of the patients I worked with, but he could have been. I had worked hard to become a skilled physical therapist, both in school and as a working professional, yet I knew very little about the severe clinical depression that often pushed our patients over the edge.

After that day on the bridge, I was determined to learn more about this problem, and once I did, I knew I had to get more involved. The stories that follow and the information I've gathered from experts are my contribution to a small but growing body of knowledge about postwar life for veterans and their caregivers. I hope that reading these stories will help more people comprehend our responsibilities as a nation to help and support not just our brave veterans of lengthy, modern-day wars, but also the spouses and families who live with and care for them.

CHAPTER 1

WHY IS MY HUSBAND SO ANGRY?
DEALING WITH POSTTRAUMATIC STRESS

The bigness of the world is redemption. Despair compresses you into a small space, and a depression is literally a hollow in the ground. To dig deeper into the self, to go underground, is sometimes necessary, but so is the other route of getting out of yourself, into the larger world, into the openness in which you need not clutch your story and your troubles so tightly to your chest.

—REBECCA SOLNIT, *The Faraway Nearby*

AFTER THE MORNING spa massage sessions at the Hotel del Coronado, the women gathered to eat lunch, sip water, and stir tea. What began as an informal conversation between a few women about the morning's relaxing activities soon evolved into something much more serious. Many of the women were now participating in a discussion that drew them all into a tight circle to comfort the storyteller.

Julie told her story through wracking sobs, one hand cradling her round face and the other raking her thick, blond hair.

"I hate Afghanistan," she said. "When Jason went over there, he was a warm, outgoing person. But he came back angry and withdrawn, and he began taking out all his anger on me and the kids."

Drawing nods of agreement and sympathetic encouragement from the others, Julie continued. "I just don't understand. I hardly recognize him. This new man fights with recurring flashbacks, rage, overprotectiveness, depression . . . It's all so hard to cope with."

Julie, like many wives of wounded warriors, felt abandoned and alone, even though she was still living with Jason. She wondered aloud why he had turned on their family—the ones he loved the most.

The other wives in the group had the same concerns. A firebrand of a woman named Jane said, "It's like we're all married to the same man with different faces, and he's having an affair with another woman."

I thought to myself that the other woman's name is Iraq or Afghanistan. She may be ugly and battle-scarred, but she still calls out to the men who know her. They can't resist her call.

Posttraumatic stress (PTS)—also known as shell shock, battle fatigue, or soldier's heart—can be described as a locked trunk full of unwept tears. Every soldier deals with the experience of combat differently. Some shut off their emotions, while others feel every moment deeply. These coping mechanisms become ingrained, and when soldiers return to their families, they find themselves numb to some feelings and oversensitive to others. Their reactions become volatile and unpredictable, swinging from alienation and betrayal to rage and regret. Often these feelings are compounded by a profound sense of survivor's grief, along with helplessness, self-pity, and anger.

One wife described her husband's PTS as a cycle.

"First he expresses it by acting out in anger," she said, "attacking an innocent person who he sees as a threat to us.

Then later, he turns it inward, shutting me out, drinking alone at bars in a deep depression. I can't convince him that he's home safe now, that there aren't any threats, or even that I love him."

PTS can affect anyone who has experienced a traumatic event such as sexual abuse, a terrorist attack, or other assaults. In life, we all face crises large and small, ranging from the loss of a cell phone to the death of a loved one. Yet these events, while stressful, aren't typically considered traumas unless we are unable to cope. A trauma is an event of such magnitude, horror, or duration that it overwhelms a person's emotional and physical coping mechanisms. The resulting traumatic stress interferes with the person's day-to-day functioning. The condition becomes a disorder when the sufferer's behavior becomes maladaptive and destructive and interferes with daily living. It's a continuum that ranges from feeling mildly depressed to being unable to get out of bed in the morning. PTS is listed in the *Diagnostic and Statistical Manual of Mental Disorders* (*DSM-5*), published by the American Psychiatric Association.

In essence, PTS is a severe reaction to an abnormal or overwhelming amount of stress. Imagine witnessing a succession of terrible car crashes, knowing there's a chance you might be the next. Or being raped twice a week for years. Even if these terrible things were not happening to you directly, imagine that they were happening to people all around you and you were powerless to stop them. What if you knew that, at any moment, you might be the next victim? Naturally, PTS is common among war veterans, but it can develop in the wives of wounded warriors, too.

PTS isn't a sign that an individual is psychologically weak, as shown by the fact that it develops in survivors of a variety of natural catastrophes, many of whom had no previous significant mental health problems. PTS can also develop in persons who witness trauma on a daily basis or are subjected to persistent and unrelieved stress as part of their jobs. This is true even for individuals who are carefully screened for mental health problems prior to admission into their fields. For example, PTS is common among rescue workers, firefighters, health care teams, and police officers. The symptoms have also been noted in prisoners of war, Holocaust survivors, and people who witnessed or were first responders to the attacks on the World Trade Center in 2001.

Sharing the stories of their husbands' PTS episodes can be crucial for wives of wounded warriors, who must learn to identify and understand PTS symptoms. These women must also learn to take steps—including getting help—to ensure the safety of their children, themselves, and the men in their lives.

Another concept that pops up on the radar while the women talk is moral injury. This might seem like it could get lumped in with PTS, but the mental health community has determined that while PTS stems from fear, moral injury has to do with an individual's sense of right and wrong. The symptoms are similar and can include depression and anxiety, difficulty paying attention, and loss of trust. But the morally injured feel sadness and regret, too. They are trying to reconcile the ethics they brought to battle with the ugliness of conflict.

As I listened to these women share their stories during lunch, I was amazed by how easily they opened up to each other. When I was going through my divorce, I had a hard time confiding in others. I felt that my troubles were just that—my troubles—and I didn't want to burden anyone else with them. I was embarrassed that my marriage hadn't worked out and didn't know how to express my feelings. If I had been more open about my struggles—taken a page out of these women's playbooks—perhaps I could have healed faster.

While the stress of my divorce was nothing compared to what these women were going through, it was heartening to witness them listen to each other and offer support. I can only imagine what a relief it must have been for these women to hear from others who were experiencing the same challenges. Connecting helped them see that they were not alone.

As the women continued sharing, it became clear to me that Julie's story had important parallels with those of other women in the group, and that they'd found the same ways to cope with their hardships. Each woman felt that living with her spouse's PTS was like being trapped in a small, stress-filled, pressurized space. Talking openly about it had, for a time, made that space bigger.

I'd like to share more of Julie's story with you, then introduce Jane, another wife from the group who reached similar conclusions about how to heal the rifts in her marriage and move beyond the pain of her husband's trauma. If you, too, are the wife of a wounded warrior, I hope their experiences and ideas can help you do the same.

JULIE: I WILL QUIET THE UNHEARD SCREAMS

"When my husband came back from his third deployment, physically and emotionally wounded, everything was different," Julie said, her voice soft and her eyes downcast. "Who was this stranger?" Jason had been shot in combat. He felt he'd gotten off easy with just an arm injury. Two of his friends had died during the attack, and he harbored a huge amount of survivor's guilt. Even though Jason couldn't talk about it, Julie felt the incident was never far from his thoughts. She came to believe that while his body might have returned, a piece of his soul was still over there.

Julie had met Jason in 2010 while they both served in the Marines. She was nineteen, stocky and tomboyish, strong like all Marines. Jason, who grew up in the South, towered above Julie at six foot two and melted her heart with his soft brown eyes. "The thing that attracted me most," Julie confessed, "was his go-to-it attitude. And the way he smelled, which was really nice."

She remembered him as a warm, fun-loving man, social and relaxed. He got along easily with friends and family, and he went out often. After they married in 2012 and had children, Jason played happily with their two young sons, Greg and Tony.

Julie came to understand that she was reconciling two very different versions of her husband. The man who returned from deployment looked just like the one she had married—tall, dark, and handsome. But he was often irritable or irrational, and he became silent and sullen with no warning, withdrawing into anxiety and depression for days. Julie would offer up ideas for outings—such as enjoying a Padres game or going out with friends for a beer—but Jason was seldom interested. She couldn't even tempt him with fishing, one of his favorite pastimes. Days turned into weeks, and his irritability and anxiety pulled him further and further inward. No matter what Julie tried, she couldn't get Jason to leave the safety of their home.

"He wouldn't make eye contact or even get out of bed. He quit shaving and showering. Nothing interested him, and we argued over little, stupid things. In all honesty, sometimes it felt like I was caring for three children instead of two," Julie told us. "He couldn't see a reason to get up every morning. He played a song, 'What's This Life For,' over and over again for what felt like months."

What had happened to Jason over the course of his three deployments? He didn't share many stories, and Julie felt shut out.

"It's really tempting to dig for the details of what happened— we're human. Heck, we're women, so we instinctively want to know *all* the details," Julie told the other wives. But she was afraid of what might happen if she prodded him too much and triggered those feelings of guilt and betrayal.

Jason's default state for emotional security was silence. Sometimes he would share what he had experienced on his deployments in small bursts, but more often he wouldn't. He just couldn't find the words. Nights were long as Julie watched his fitful sleep. She could still remember what it felt like to be wrapped up in his strong arms, but now she felt empty and abandoned.

Julie was able to face those long nights and silent days because of a deeply held belief that things would get better with time. She played the song "I Won't Give Up on You" by Jason Mraz to remind her husband that she was there to support him. She asked him to go to therapy at the VA. It took a while to persuade him, but eventually Jason agreed. As they walked into their first session together, Julie took his enormous hand in her own and told him she wouldn't give up on him so long as he didn't give up on himself.

The therapist listened without judgment and inquired about Jason's obsession with the song that asked, "What's this life for?" The therapist couldn't give Jason a meaning and purpose to life, but by asking the right questions he helped Jason find those things for himself and find reasons to get up most mornings.

Julie related some of the things Jason shared about his combat memories in these sessions. "The first time I killed was a high. This fucker was going to kill us, but I killed him instead."

Good therapists understand that they don't always know what's best for their clients, and help normalize traumatic experiences by saying, "How did you have the strength to respond that way?" and, "I don't see how you could have done anything different at that time."

Eventually, Jason opened up about the events surrounding his injury and the trauma he'd experienced. He revealed that he had been part of the group responsible for training the Afghan police.

It had been a long, hot, stressful week of training and patrol. Jason was daydreaming about being safe at home and jumping into the ocean; he missed his freedom and couldn't wait to get out of that shithole. Those were his exact thoughts, he told the counselor, when he heard a bang. His body clenched and stiffened. He turned around. One of the members of the Afghan police they'd been training had turned his gun on his comrades.

Bloodlust coursed through Jason's veins as he sprang into action. He was shot trying to stop the "insider" attack from injuring or killing more of his friends. He didn't even feel the bullet as it pierced his right shoulder and shredded his right arm.

Jason lost two of his closest friends in the attack. He lived the nightmare of seeing his best friends killed. In his mind, he replayed the episode over and over. He also grappled with self-doubt: Had he reacted too slowly? Could he have done something more to save his buddies? Why didn't he see the attack coming?

Jason's experience isn't unusual and, in light of what he experienced, it's understandable that he would struggle to downshift into civilian life. Everyone who has been deployed to a war zone is changed by his or her experience; it would be abnormal not to be. The journey of readjusting after combat is one of learning to live with traumatic experiences and integrate them into postwar life, without blaming oneself for what did or didn't happen. Wounded warriors must retrain themselves to communicate, and it's a long, painstaking process. They must figure out how to react to situations as nonwarriors, even try to reclaim a little bit of who they were before they *became* warriors.

"Jason does his best with our boys, but he gets aggravated a lot faster than he used to," Julie said. "So when he brought home *Why Is Dad So Mad?* by Seth Kastle, it meant a lot to me. Just him reading that book to the kids was a big help, and everything in it is pretty much true about Jason. [Those passages] helped the boys better understand what was happening with their own dad."

Jason received a prosthetic arm, and after a year of occupational therapy he felt able to leave the house, but only on his really good days. As he gradually became more social and visible, Julie began encountering another kind of frustration: people who knew nothing about their situation would sometimes sit in judgment. "He seems just fine to me," she would hear, or, "He was normal the last time I saw him." Other friends and family would accuse him of faking his condition, saying things like, "He has a new arm now. Can't he just get on with it?"

For Jason, this wave of unfeeling, unthinking remarks inflicted new, invisible wounds. For Julie, the harsh comments were stunning at first, but she soon learned to consider them a blessing. The way people responded to her husband's condition often revealed their true character, underlying ignorance, or lack of ability to be supportive. Just as we slow down and look carefully when we approach a flashing light at an intersection, Julie learned to assess possible emotional collisions and steer clear of certain individuals.

Even as Jason was progressing in his recovery, Julie realized she needed more support for herself. She reached out to a number of service organizations, including a group that held caregiver meetings at the Vet Center. She discovered that other women were experiencing similar frustrations. She wasn't alone in her struggles. The group referred her to the Operation Family Caregiver program, where she learned problem-solving techniques. One of Julie's looming worries was that she didn't have an exit strategy if Jason eventually *did* give up on himself. She had drawn a line in the sand, saying she would leave if he didn't truly commit to therapy and his healing processes, but she wasn't sure she could support herself if it came down to that.

A counselor shored up her confidence and helped her find full-time work so she could make good on her ultimatum. If her husband quit going to group and individual therapy, she could and would leave.

Through her own therapy, Julie also learned how to accept and cope with this new, different Jason. First she addressed her husband's silence. She learned that when he became silent, it wasn't something she should take personally. She came to understand Jason's need to process information at his own rate, and that forcing him to share details before he was ready could hinder his recovery. Instead of feeling frustrated, she opted to cultivate her patience.

As difficult as the dark days were, moments of light did begin to grace Julie's life. She became the top salesperson at her local sports store and started teaching fly-fishing classes. She even learned how to tie flies. In time, she found her own ways of staying centered. Simple practices such as venting with friends, listening to music, taking a drive, or going shopping helped her stay calm and maintain her sanity throughout this difficult period. An unexpected side effect of her experience was that she learned what she was made of, as a wife and as a person.

"You never really know what you have in you until something brings it out of you," she mused.

Now that Julie had the added responsibility of being the primary breadwinner—on top of caregiving, mothering, cooking, cleaning, and shopping for the family—she realized she was capable of juggling more than she'd ever imagined. Although she had retired from the Marines long ago when she found out she was pregnant, her military career had given her confidence and organizational skills she could tap into as she cared for Jason.

"I discovered that I am a *very* patient and easygoing person," Julie said. "It's not an easy job to take care of two kids and another adult, but I make it happen to keep our family together, like it should be."

Just as a long, rainy day has moments when the rain subsides, so did the emotionally rainy days of Julie's life. She didn't take a single sunburst for granted. If some friends were getting together for a short getaway, she was definitely game so long as she could find help with childcare. (Jason could only watch the kids for brief periods of time.) If Jason was having a good day, she was *all* his and enjoyed just spending time with her family. She had made a successful transition into civilian life and knew, deep down, that he could too.

On one of her getaway days fly-fishing, Julie learned about Project Healing Waters, a program dedicated to the physical and emotional rehabilitation of disabled veterans through fly-fishing and related activities. Recalling Jason's lifelong love of fishing, she signed both of them up for a Healing Waters retreat.

"Fly-fishing with the love of my life on a quiet river brought back our flow," Julie said. "These quickly became the moments we valued the most. Jason became certified as a fly-fishing instructor, and I worked as a guide during the summers. It allowed our family to get away from it all in nature."

Learning to tie flies (he can tie them with one hand) and cast taught Jason to adapt to his injuries and gave him a new skill he could be proud of. He didn't think he'd ever find anything as meaningful as bonding with his comrades in the military, but Julie's encouragement inspired him to be curious and try new things. Although he'd fished, Jason never had an interest in fly-fishing until his wife introduced it to him. Sharing her passion brought them closer together.

Today, Julie is hopeful about the future as both she and Jason continue certification courses to make fly-fishing instruction a full-time career. The Project Healing Waters program is international now, and the couple plans to follow the world's waterways to other veterans. Jason feels as though he's moving in a new direction after his military career and his healing is an example of hope for others.

"Going out on the water and forgetting about Afghanistan even for just a few days satisfies my soul," he explained to Julie.

Now when the world gets too stressful, Jason knows he has other options besides retreating into solitude and depression. Being on the water gives him a feeling of belonging in the universe, and that connection is crucial. He no longer wonders if there's a point to living when he's fly-fishing with Julie.

"It's just us, the water, and the fish," Julie said. "Helping other veterans learn to fly-fish has given us both new meaning, purpose, and peace."

JANE: I WILL HEAL YOUR SHATTERED SOUL

Jane is older than many other wives of wounded warriors. The passionate redhead is in her forties, while the other wives are typically in their twenties and early thirties. But when Jane, whose lively personality endears her to everyone she meets, relates her wounded warrior's story, everyone finds it all too familiar. She is deeply connected to the others despite their age difference.

She met her husband Kyle while they were working as forest rangers at Vail Mountain, Colorado. He was a big guy, bald and blue-eyed, with an appealingly athletic build and a personality to match. Jane was an outdoorsy person herself, and they fell in love hiking in the summer and skiing in the winter. They were engaged six months after they met and married six months later, in October 1990. Kyle was in the U.S. Navy Reserve at the time, doing his duty on weekends and for two weeks a year. Then, after they had been married nearly twenty years, Kyle was put on active duty and required to leave for longer periods. That's when the anxiety started.

"Usually it wasn't too bad, because I was working full time, taking care of our two kids and my mom," Jane said. "So I was very busy on the home front. Kyle wasn't going anywhere near the war at that time, so I felt he was safe. But in June of 2010, he was sent to Afghanistan, and then I got scared. Our daughter was getting married, and we moved the wedding up so her daddy could walk her down the aisle. It felt so grim to make that decision, but we didn't know what to expect. What if he never came back?" She furrowed her freckled brow as she related this painful memory.

After only a few weeks in Afghanistan, Kyle's Humvee was hit by an explosion from an IED, and both of his legs had to be amputated. He was lucky to be medically evacuated within the first hour of his injuries, or the consequences would have been much worse. After bilateral amputations above the knees, he was told he'd eventually be fitted with new legs and that he would have to go through intense physical therapy for two years.

Jane thought that once he completed therapy, their life together would be smoother. She didn't notice the aftershocks of PTS and traumatic brain injury (TBI) until after Kyle was discharged and had been home for quite some time.

She told her pastor, family, and friends that she felt sure something was wrong because Kyle was acting so differently. His quick temper and frequent nightmares worried her. He often got dizzy and had ringing in his ears; his eyes became light-sensitive, which forced him to wear dark glasses all the time; he was very distressed by noise and could not be around crowds. His mood swings were epic, taking him from sullen to furious in a matter of seconds, and he seemed agitated and anxious all day, every day.

"When work suspended him for ninety days because of a major mistake, I knew something was wrong," Jane recalled. "I was worried about his health, what had happened, and why he wasn't telling me anything."

After Kyle's suspension, Jane used her fiery Irish powers of persuasion to convince him to get help. She was so relieved when he called the local veterans center and went in for an evaluation.

"The counselor was wonderful and knew just how to get through the VA system," Jane said. "Kyle asked me to come to an appointment with him, and that's when I finally heard about all that had happened to him. I started crying and asked why he hadn't shared this with me sooner. He told me he didn't want me to worry. Well, now I was *really* worried about his health and unsure if he would be okay."

With the help of the counselor, Kyle began to uncover and discuss some of his most traumatic experiences in battle. "The vehicle in front of us was destroyed by an IED, so we established security and called the medic," Kyle said. "Once security was established, a second IED detonated approximately twenty meters from my location and directly under where I had just been standing. Then a third IED detonated."

Kyle and his men returned fire, but it was chaos on the scene. He said he felt helpless and confused, since he couldn't see the enemy through all the smoke and had no idea where the triggerman was hiding.

"Killing the enemy is what I was trained to do, but I couldn't identify who the enemy was. I was hit and don't remember much else, though I know I was firing into the blast area and definitely hit a few men. I go over the events again and again in my mind. Did I kill an innocent person or did I kill the triggerman?"

Once she understood the scope of Kyle's trauma, Jane sought support in her faith. Her church community stepped up and provided her with prayers and a quiet, safe space for contemplation. Jane also felt very lucky that her family understood when her husband needed special care, and that their friends were flexible when Jane and Kyle had to decline invitations because Kyle would be uncomfortable around crowds and noise. She took it upon herself to study up on PTS to gain a better understanding of what triggered Kyle's outbursts and to develop strategies for heading them off, removing him from situations that caused him anxiety or stress. For example, at a church potluck, Kyle started to yell at people he thought were talking too loudly. Jane quickly realized that he was being overstimulated and gently guided him back home.

But Jane found that her husband's PTS took a psychological toll on her as well. She would get depressed because she couldn't always do the things she wanted to do. Sometimes she would cope in unhealthy ways, such as eating more and not going to the gym. Self-care can fall by the wayside when all of your time and energy get used up caring for someone else. And although Jane believed they had a strong marriage, she eventually saw that his injuries had changed how they treated each other.

"We still are very close and love each other very much," she said. "But I feel I have to leave the room at times because of things he says or does."

One of the most noticeable changes to Jane was Kyle's temper. When he became angry, he had no filter when he spoke. She had to painstakingly explain to him how some of the unfiltered things he said made her feel, because he couldn't seem to process her reactions without an explanation.

"He has emotionally regressed," Jane confided. "He's not the man he used to be. Sometimes I feel like I'm dealing with a two-year-old throwing a temper tantrum."

She learned that when her husband lost control of his emotions, it was important for her to stay in control. She had to recognize that she was dealing with someone under an extreme amount of stress. If he acted out violently, she gave herself permission to leave, but she also found ways to navigate tense situations with Kyle. Through group therapy, she acquired tools for staying centered under stressful conditions and learned how to set boundaries.

Jane knows she's learned and grown through the hard times, and she gives this advice to younger women: "Don't let them go through this alone. Get help fast for your loved one *and* for yourself. But also find something that you can do alone that will help you relax. Be patient and loving, and try to understand what your wounded warrior is going through. Learn as much as you can about PTS."

Grateful that she'd had the chance to travel when she was younger, Jane became content to stay home and care for her husband and grandkids. She believed her best tool was her even temperament, which helped defuse situations within her marriage that could otherwise have become explosive.

Jane laughed as she contemplated this easygoing side of her personality. "When I was younger, I was a bit of a hothead myself. But age has mellowed me, so I can go with the flow in certain situations."

Even though Jane was resigned to not traveling or going on adventures, she missed that part of her life. So in early 2015, when Kyle told her about the Vail Veterans Program, they packed their bags in the blink of an eye.

The Vail Veterans Program was founded in 2004 to provide rehabilitation sports training to severely wounded warriors and their wives. Jane was excited about this organization because although it was focused on helping her husband heal, she got to participate too.

As you might expect of a program based in Vail, this one was all about skiing. Kyle's instructors strapped him into a monoski and put him on Golden Peak's bunny hill. Jane skied alongside him and watched him open up and transform before her eyes. This program got him out of his shell and rekindled their shared love of the outdoors.

"Gliding through the snow on 'wings of wood' is the closest thing to flying," Jane explained. "We felt so free soaring over the slopes."

The healing process is a journey that lasts a lifetime for wounded warriors and for their caregivers. But the four days Jane spent with Kyle in Vail, skiing and sharing meals with other wounded warriors and their wives, were a turning point in both of their lives. Now these two are healing their wounded souls through sharing new positive experiences and gently forcing a world that can feel small and suffocating to expand and unfold.

As a physical therapist working with patients in rehabilitation, I have seen how most patients can't wait to get out into the great outdoors after being in a hospital for months. I've taken patients skiing, fishing, hiking, and horseback riding, and have witnessed their eyes light up as they experience the world beyond the hospital room.

Getting away from the hospital is as beneficial for the wives as it is for our patients. The desire to escape can seem irresponsible, but at times it's essential. The wives can't "suit up and show up" day after day without ever taking a break. There are times when they must face their responsibilities, and dodging them is not the answer. But every once in a while, they need to break free.

Sometimes the best thing they can do for themselves is run like hell—as fast and as far away as they can possibly go— because there are circumstances in which a change of scenery can change their minds. There are times when spending time away from the hospital, away from the city, away from the stress, can be just the balm their wounded souls need. And when they feel trapped in the stifling space of a home filled with angry outbursts, flashbacks, and night terrors, leaving home *together* can be the key to unlocking a whole new level of recovery and reconciliation. Taking the running leap of going to Vail together offered Kyle and Jane a better chance of learning to fly.

CHAPTER 2

TRAUMATIC BRAIN INJURY: MY HUSBAND'S MIND AND MEMORY HIJACKED

There is no greater agony than holding an untold story inside you.

—MAYA ANGELOU

MANY OF THE wives who gather at SPA Days tell me that the invisible injuries their husbands incur are often the hardest to cope with. PTS is almost universal in wounded warriors and brings chaos and confusion into their homes, but TBI sometimes wreaks even more havoc on unprepared families.

"I honestly had no idea what I was in for when I heard the diagnosis," said Cindy, a sweet strawberry blond with an equally sweet Southern drawl. "Our lives changed forever."

Shannon, a polished, professional, platinum-blond woman, added, "Nothing is more painful than seeing your man in pain and not being able to comfort him because he's so out of it, so far gone."

TBI can occur when the head is hit with significant force. Whether it comes from the head hitting the windshield during a car accident, impact from a fall, or trauma from a nearby explosion during military service, TBI can significantly affect many areas of a person's life, creating changes in physical functioning, cognition, and behavior.

According to 2015 Pentagon data, one in five veterans returning from war suffers from TBI at various levels of severity. These injuries range from mild concussions—"getting your bell rung"—to severe comas. Mild TBI is associated with brief changes in or loss of consciousness, and some wounded warriors with mild TBI have been able to return to active duty. Others who have suffered severe TBI cannot return to service. While it might be easier to diagnose moderate to severe TBI, changes caused by any TBI can have a huge impact on many areas of a person's life.

The first hours after a TBI are shocking and terrifying for everyone involved. Wounded soldiers sometimes arrive home for medical care in comas, swathed in gauze, and covered in tubes. Their wives or parents face immediate, life-altering decisions, such as whether to amputate a shattered leg, how long to keep a loved one on life support, and whether the body will be donated to medical science should the soldier die. They often don't comprehend the significance of TBI until after their wounded warrior is out of the hospital. Young wives in their twenties pour their resilience and dedication into becoming full-time caregivers for their husbands, not realizing that they'll be filling that role for decades to come, as they both age into their seventies and beyond. These men look but no longer behave like the husbands they once knew so well.

"He was like an infant; he was so drugged up and so dopey," Katy said, remembering the first time she saw her husband Bryan in the hospital after he'd been wounded. "We didn't have any idea of what was going to happen."

How could they?

A decade ago, no one anticipated that the wars in Iraq and Afghanistan would produce so many battle casualties. Among them are young Americans ripped out of the hands of death by advanced trauma care, and many of them now require lifelong assistance. Battle training and preparation are lavished on combat-bound military personnel, but there is no training for managing the realities of being severely wounded. Not for the combat troops. Not for their families.

Newcomers to this daunting and murky world often don't understand that military medicine is terrific at addressing immediate problems—patching holes, repairing crushed bones, grafting skin and muscle, healing the stump of an amputated limb—but not as effective at dealing with the long-term physical and psychological consequences of severe wounds. Few families anticipate that those consequences could persist or even increase over a long lifetime. And it's certainly not widely known that the primary responsibility for taking care of these long-term problems gradually shifts from the professional military and VA staff to families, particularly to wives and mothers.

For those left to care for severely wounded or disabled soldiers over time, the stress can become severe. Caregivers and medical professionals say that it isn't uncommon to feel trapped in their hopeless lives and to eventually feel that suicide is the only way to escape.

"We've all thought it," said Jane. "That the only way out is to kill yourself. You fought so hard, but there comes a point where it seems you can't live like that anymore, and there's nowhere to turn—it gets so bad."

"One of the things everyone ignores is that there's a life afterward," Shannon said, rubbing the back of her neck with her manicured hand. "After doctors at Walter Reed tended to Tyler's immediate wounds, we didn't know what to do with the rest of our lives."

The good news is that we are saving more lives, due to advanced trauma care and the ability to medically evacuate the injured from the battlefield. The VA might be a bureaucracy-heavy institution, but it is constantly improving. Systems run better now than they did fifteen years ago, and support for veterans is more advanced in the U.S. than in many other countries.

But in my years of creating physical therapy regimens for patients, I've discovered that institutions don't heal patients; individuals do. No matter how many more advances the VA makes, care for a wounded warrior coping with a brain injury ultimately will continue to fall upon his spouse or caregiver. These strong, patient, giving women are the unsung heroes, standing on the sidelines after the medals have been awarded, the parades have ended, and our soldiers finally emerge from the hospital, their lives forever changed.

In the stories that follow, Shannon and Katy relate how their marriages changed after their husbands came home from battle with TBIs. Both women found themselves moving from self-sufficiency and independence to reliance on family, humor, introspection, and the support of their communities to rebuild their lives. Both believe they've emerged from difficult recoveries feeling stronger than ever, within themselves and within their marriages.

SHANNON: NOTHING ELSE MATTERS

Would you ever think that the hardest day of your life could also be your happiest? Shannon couldn't have predicted this for herself, but it turned out to be true. The day Tyler—her toweringly tall, hot, Irish husband—came home injured was the hardest day she'd ever lived through. She was five months pregnant with their first child, and had spent his deployment teaching her grade-schoolers and thinking of every single day as "one day closer to Tyler coming home."

When Shannon first met Tyler in 2002, she had just started her teaching career and he was an Army sergeant. A warm, gregarious man, Tyler took great pride in his job and in "his" men. He loved sharing stories about his experiences in the Army, punctuating them with booming laughter and with a mischievous twinkle in his dark green eyes. Shannon was a knockout herself—a Gwen Stefani lookalike—and they made a handsome, happy couple.

She used to wait eagerly for Tyler to come home from work. Every day was the same. He'd come up the outside stairs and look through the kitchen window and see her there. He'd wink and smile, then plow through the door and come right up to her, hug her tightly, give her a kiss, and say, "Hey, babe, how was your day?"

His passion for cooking and wine led them to epicurean delights when he was home from deployments. He was everything to her since the moment they started dating.

Shannon remembered the day of his return home with a shudder. At 10:30 on what seemed like an ordinary Tuesday morning, she got a phone call that still chilled her to the bone when she told it to the group of women.

"Is this Mrs. Riley? I have information about your husband." Words seemed to roll off the caller's tongue with the casual tone of someone placing an order at a restaurant.

What transpired after that quickly turned what should have been a happy reunion into a living nightmare. Shannon was caught in a whirlwind of emotions, vacillating between feeling hopeful and hopeless, angry and grateful. He was still alive and so were the other guys. Knowing that should have brought relief, but relief wasn't one of the emotions she could tap.

Have you ever had a single, memorable moment that forever changed your life? You finally got your dream job, met the person you were going to marry, had a baby or watched one be born, or said good-bye to a precious loved one? Those are moments that are forever etched in your mind. For Shannon, her life-changing moment was receiving the phone call and learning that Tyler—who had been deployed on January 1, 2005, for his second tour of combat duty in Iraq—had been injured on May 15. An IED in a suicide vehicle detonated under an overpass where he was standing post. He and seven other soldiers were injured in the incident. Tyler's injuries were among the worst. He sustained a massive head injury along with several broken bones. He was medically evacuated and spent time in four different medical stations before finally being sent back home to the U.S., where he would spend the next eighteen months in recovery.

When Shannon finally reunited with Tyler in the hospital, he was unable to speak or move, and barely registered her presence. She was devastated, but steeled herself for whatever might come next. As soon as he was stable enough, Shannon installed herself at the hospital by Tyler's side. During rehabilitation at Walter Reed Army Medical Center, he received six hours daily of physical therapy, occupational therapy, speech therapy, and psychiatric consultation.

"For the first two months I waited for any visible change in his state or behavior," Shannon said. "I waited for him to acknowledge me with a hand squeeze, an eyeblink, a smile, anything to let me know he recognized me."

When one nurse told Shannon that he wouldn't wake up

and she needed to accept his vegetative state, she shrugged it off, focused on his warrior determination, and told herself he would pull through. His physical therapist encouraged her to play his favorite music, bring in photos of his preinjury days, and provide all the stimulation of sight, smell, touch, and sound that could help him orientate to place and time and remember his life and family. The doctors encouraged her to speak to him as if he understood everything she said.

Months passed, and eventually hope and optimism turned to anger and despair. During those dark days in the hospital room, Shannon dwelled on how she resented Tyler and hated herself for feeling that way. She resented him for putting himself in a position to become this badly injured, and for denying her and their unborn child his amazing, strong, loving former self. She resented him for the family vacations they would never take together. She watched friends travel with their families, making wonderful memories, but even her preinjury vacation pictures were always missing Tyler. And she resented him for leaving her behind to fight instead of showing her the love that he'd said he felt for her. Was it horrible to resent a person for things that were completely out of his control? She knew it was, but she desperately wanted the life they had promised each other.

Then, in a moment of clarity, she stopped, considered everything she was feeling, and realized he hadn't let her down at all. He had put himself in that position because he loved what he did, and he loved his country. He loved helping others and would drop anything and everything for his comrades. That was one of the things she loved best about him. She realized that he hadn't joined her on their vacations because of his brave and admirable commitment to the United States. He had wanted to be part of something big and important, and sadly, he had become horribly wounded while doing it.

The day Shannon's water broke she was already at the hospital, lifting Tyler off of the commode onto his wheelchair.

She hadn't slowed down one bit as she neared her due date, and she drew upon her seemingly endless stores of inner strength to make it through those last uncomfortable months, caring for Tyler all the while. As they sat in the bathroom together, she talked about what was to happen and could see a tiny sparkle in his bleary eyes. Her heart brimming, she was rushed to delivery and gave birth to a healthy eight-pound girl. Shannon cut the umbilical cord herself and listened to the strong, strident cries of her beautiful new child. She could sense determination and inner fire in the tiny infant, and it gave her hope. As she cradled her baby girl, she knew that, at this point, she could do anything. Fearlessly, together with this new addition to their little family, they would all learn to thrive, not just survive.

During her very first visit with her daddy, this amazing baby made it clear that her arrival would change everything. The miracle of her birth was just the beginning. When the nurse wheeled Shannon and their newborn daughter into Tyler's room, another miracle happened. He smiled. They named their daughter Hope, after the moment they came to think of as Tyler's "waking up."

After that, everything did change. Shannon rededicated herself to encouraging Tyler's recovery, and Tyler finally began to show improvement. After months of stagnation, he began regaining language he'd lost when he sustained his brain injury.

The next big milestone for Tyler was learning to walk again, which he did slowly but steadily through physical therapy. He began relearning daily living activities through occupational therapy. He worked on restoring his speech, short-term and long-term memory, and problem-solving skills through cognitive training and speech therapy. Shannon never gave up on Tyler, and she found a physical therapist who wouldn't, either. In fact, she changed therapists until she found a whole team that believed he could recover and that would support him through the process.

Shannon learned she could win over hospital staff by bringing a weekly box of See's candies to the nurse's station and fancy coffee for the therapists. She was assertive, always asking for the best therapists, but she always posed her requests in a kind way. If she couldn't be there, she made sure a friend or family member was at Tyler's side to watch and learn about his treatments, as well as to make sure those treatments were never cancelled.

Her perseverance paid off. A year and a half after sustaining his injury, Tyler walked.

Swim therapy helped with his spasticity, and he began to regain coordination and strength. Shannon and Tyler found ways to laugh about everything, as his gregarious personality returned along with his memory. One day the therapist was helping him swim, showing the doctors how his spasticity was decreasing and mobility increasing. He took one big backstroke and knocked the therapist's swimsuit off. It took the therapist a moment to notice, but Tyler choked on the pool water from laughing so hard.

Shannon took maternity leave for a year to care for their daughter, but when Tyler was discharged from the hospital she knew her profession was a lifeline to her strength. She loved teaching, and that passion kept her life going. In September 2008, once she knew that Tyler was in a good place and making progress, she returned to the classroom. She knew she wasn't abandoning him; she was caring for herself.

Tyler was equally determined and self-reliant. Never one to depend solely on others, he made some big changes when he was discharged. He focused his steely, military determination on rebuilding his body and worked out in his home gym to gain back his strength and independence. He refused to take disability pay and instead became a wine broker. He turned his passion for the beautiful epicurean life into a job that focused on food and wine. Traveling the country, visiting vineyards, and learning about drinking trends, he distributed wines to both restaurants and liquor stores.

"I could have accepted disability and stayed home, but I refused," he explained, writing out his thoughts. "My life is about overcoming adversity and being productive to prove to the world I matter."

Tyler's determination and inner fire set an example for Hope that is even more meaningful now that she's nearly ten years old. He taught his daughter how to be strong, how to persevere, how to fight for what she wants, how to be grateful for the gift of being alive, and how to put others ahead of herself. And every time he reaches his hand out to Shannon and gives her a grin, she's grateful she stayed strong through their tragedy.

Shannon revealed to us that we happened to be gathering for SPA Day on the anniversary of the day Tyler was injured.

"Today, like every year on this day, I look at my man and thank God that I can still kiss his face and tell him how much I love him," she told us, tearing up. "I look at the relationships I have now because of the injuries Tyler has sustained, and am in awe of the amazing people I have met and that are now part of our lives. I look at the amazing girl that we are raising and imagine the woman she will become."

She told us that she considers the other seven men injured alongside Tyler to be family, and that she's so proud of all they have accomplished. They are the military family that will always have a place in her biological family's hearts.

Shannon expressed her gratitude for all of the opportunities she has been given—to tell her story, to help other caregivers, and to share everything with her new friends when she speaks at SPA Days.

"These women are what keep me going in this very difficult life," she explained. "They're the ones who 'get it' and the ones I never have to apologize to if I'm late, if plans change, or if I simply want to be angry at God. I'm also very thankful to my friends that have been there for me since the beginning, the ones that care enough to make sure that I'm still a part of their lives.

It's these people," she continued, "who know I'm more than someone who tends to Tyler's injuries. They allow me to be me and love me for it."

Shannon quoted the Rolling Stones lyric, "You can't always get what you want, but if you try sometimes, you just might find you get what you need." Shannon and Tyler didn't ask for this injury, but they believe they have gotten what they need. They have an amazing support system that continues to help with ongoing doctor appointments, childcare, and medical bills. It's a support system that Shannon admits she needs. Without it, she would not be able to continue to handle her complicated life every day—especially on the anniversary of her husband's injury.

"That day was the hardest day of my life, and I hate how it completely flipped our lives upside down," she explained, her voice thick with tears. "But today, like every day, I try to focus on the positives of what life has to offer us. I will continue to do everything in my power to make sure that Tyler and I stay independent, healthy, and happy, and that he knows that I love him just as much today as I did the day I married him. I'll remind him that he is still my everything and he will always be, and that I am one lucky woman to still have him in my life."

Shannon named the day of his injury "Alive Day," the day his life was saved. And whenever that bittersweet anniversary rolls around, she makes a point of telling him, "Happy Alive Day, my sweet, sweet man."

KATY: NOT OKAY

The phone rang, breaking Katy's already restless sleep. She rubbed her dark brown eyes and pushed her thin, black hair away from her face. She had barely gotten her two children to bed and, just before she'd finally drifted off to sleep, her mind had been on her husband Bryan, who was serving as a corpsman and medic in the Marines in western Afghanistan. She hadn't heard from him in over a week, and when they hadn't spoken in a while, her imagination took over and led her to a dark place.

She fumbled for the phone by her bedside, uttering some sort of hello while glancing at the clock. It was 11:00 p.m.

"Is this Mrs. Brown?"

"Yes, this is she."

"I'm calling from Bagram Base."

Katy pushed the covers away from her wiry frame and stood up. "Oh my God. Is Bryan okay?"

The caller identified himself as an officer and proceeded to deliver the news that had prompted the late-night call.

"Ma'am, I can tell you that your husband's Humvee was hit by an IED on the eighth day of a ten-day mission. He will be coming home early. And, yes, overall, he's okay."

With only a few more quick words, the officer hung up the phone. Katy had been too stunned to respond, but as soon as the officer hung up, a million questions collided in her mind. How soon would Bryan be coming home? How badly was he hurt? And what did "overall, he's okay" mean exactly?

"That scared me," Katy told the group, recalling that night. "I was incredibly confused and overwhelmed by the scenarios that began running through my mind. I didn't know what to do."

Though exhausted, Katy could not return to sleep. She sat there in the blue cool of the night, holding the phone in her hand, trying to push the darkest thoughts away and cling to hope. Somewhere deep down, she knew that this was a dividing line kind of moment, and nothing would ever be the same. The life she knew before the phone call was gone, and her life afterward was irrevocably changed. She just didn't know how.

Katy had met Bryan in 2006 while they were working at a Lake Tahoe ski resort. Both were in their early twenties, had dropped out of college, and were lovers of the great outdoors. As ski season came to an end, they moved to Alaska to work at Denali National Park. They spent their time hiking, exploring, and occasionally dodging curious bears and moose. Their adventurous natures made them a perfect match.

Bryan was a trained paramedic and was working a mountain safety job at Denali when a Marine recruiter approached him. He was such a natural at dealing with trauma—able to keep a clear head in any crisis—that the military seemed like a perfect fit. His first deployment rolled around quicker than expected, and Bryan nudged Katy about getting married before he left. After that, things moved fast. Katy discovered she was pregnant while Bryan was at boot camp. They tied the knot in January 2007, and he shipped out in February.

Katy and Bryan made the most of their time together between deployments, having another adorable baby and moving from base to base. Then in 2012 came the orders for a thirteen-month deployment to Afghanistan, and Katy found herself scared for Bryan's safety more than ever before. Only a few months into that deployment, she got the late-night phone call that brought all of her worst nightmares to life.

When Bryan was brought to Balboa Naval Hospital in San Diego, he was confined to the intensive care unit. He'd suffered multiple broken bones (including both femurs), a dislocated knee, a fractured thoracic vertebra, and a TBI. When Katy first saw Bryan, she was shocked. Huge rods had created cages around both of his legs. Until he had surgery, screws going through to the bone kept his legs from moving. He wore a hard shell around his chest and back to stabilize his vertebrae. He also had a cast on his broken right foot. He hadn't been bathed since his injury; he had refused to let anyone wash him but Katy.

"In that moment I felt frozen in time," she said. "But then he smiled at me, and for a minute all I could be was thankful."

As Katy pressed the staff and officers for details, a picture of what had happened to Bryan began to form. A 240-pound IED had devastated his Humvee. The vehicle flipped over four times before it finally rolled to a stop. It caught fire and its doors jammed, so Bryan had to escape through the turret bowl.

When Katy bathed him, she had to get in the hospital shower with him. She felt clumsy and awkward trying to wash his broken body and sandy-brown buzz cut with nothing separating her and her husband from the nurses on duty but a thin, translucent curtain. She was so nervous that she fumbled with the soap and dropped it. She longed for the day when Bryan would be released from the hospital and she could bathe him in the comfort and privacy of their own home.

But Bryan ended up being in intensive care for a month, and remained hospitalized for several months after that while recovering from his injuries. In what world is that "overall, okay"? Katy often thought. And when the day finally came for Bryan to go home, a new kind of shock set in.

"Coming home was a wake-up call," Katy said. "It was actually easier to care for Bryan while he was in the hospital. I had no idea it would be that way."

The extent of Bryan's TBI didn't reveal itself until he tried to get back to living a normal life. In the hospital, nobody had gauged how bad the damage really was.

"He had a really difficult time remembering things and couldn't do all the things he'd done before his injury. He couldn't read or drive, and he needed help bathing and getting dressed. He had a hard time concentrating, and sometimes his vision would change."

Even walking was out of the question, since he was still

confined to a wheelchair while his wounds healed. All of this had an immediate impact on their daily lives.

"Every time I left the house," Katy explained, "I had to get the kids into a stroller and Bryan into his chair. Everything we did took almost three times longer than it had before."

Katy already had her hands full, with two little children to take care of and a house to maintain. She didn't know when she'd find the time to be there for Bryan as he went through his rehabilitation program. But she soon realized the solution was simple: "You make time."

The physical changes were trying, but the psychological challenges were even more daunting. Suddenly their roles had changed and, at times, reversed. Bryan had always been Katy's protector, the strong man of the house, but now she was the one protecting and caring for him. His physical injuries prevented him from feeling independent, and his TBI left him a little slower to respond physically but quicker to anger, which was a recipe for disaster when they left the house.

To cope with her new daily challenges, Katy adopted a number of strategies to help her get through the tough days and long nights. Her "go-to" tool for staying strong and sane was to have a sense of humor about everything.

"You have to go with the flow and not go crazy and pull out your hair when you're having a bad day," she said with a lopsided grin.

Bryan did his best to be lighthearted, too, especially when the whole family was together. One time he was playing with the kids, and he started chasing them around in his wheelchair. They ran circles around him and he couldn't catch them. Eventually, he forgot why he was chasing them and stopped. They all piled onto his wheelchair and gave him big hugs.

"When you're caring for someone with severe physical and brain injuries, humor goes a long way," Katy said. "Take it from me."

Finding comedy in tragedy can be essential to the coping process.

Another lesson Katy had to learn was that when someone offers to help, you should accept it gracefully. She hated feeling like a charity case, even when she knew the assistance would make her life more manageable. Although she worked hard to maintain a positive outlook, Katy still struggled with the complexity of her new life. In addition to dealing with increased worry, responsibility, and stress in her life, she also found herself mourning the loss of the able-bodied man that she had married. Whether he liked it or not, Bryan had to depend on Katy more than ever. His physical therapy and rehabilitation were going fantastically, and the effects of his TBI were miraculously beginning to fade, but life was far from easy.

Katy didn't want to rely on or burden anyone outside the family, but eventually she realized that she simply didn't have all the answers. She recognized the importance of getting help, and in 2014 she connected with the Southern Caregiver Resource Center and wives of wounded warriors support groups, where she could commiserate with others going through similar situations. When she couldn't be strong all on her own, she was able to draw strength from these people, with whom she could cry without feeling guilty afterward. Her counselors and fellow wives taught her yet more coping methods to help her work through her grief, to find that kernel of resilience that would keep her going.

"When I tell my story to the others in the support group, we feel a collective sigh of relief. There is tremendous comfort in laughing and crying together."

Katy also drew comfort from knowing that she would eventually pay forward the support and guidance she was receiving. "Chances are you will be there one day for others in need," she explained. "So if you fall on hard times and someone offers to watch your kids, clean your house, or bring you dinner, accept that kindness with open arms. Let humanity do its thing!"

Through these support systems, Katy learned that self-care was nonnegotiable. She had to take care of herself, eat right, and get rest. Otherwise, she wouldn't have the strength and stamina to take care of her husband and children.

"Sometimes it's as simple as talking to a friend, having a cup of tea, or just going for a walk around the block," she said.

For Bryan, regaining resilience was a process he explored through the physical. As his recovery sped along, he began to bike to strengthen his legs, started skiing again, and even took up fly-fishing. He rebuilt his physical and psychological strength through action.

But for Katy, emotional resilience was all about attitude. By focusing on what she was grateful for, she was able to find solutions to problems rather than dwelling on the negative. She was grateful that her husband came home alive, completed his three-year rehabilitation, and even that he was able to return to active duty in 2015. All it took was a quick gratitude check to get her attitude where it needed to be.

That might sound difficult, and it is. "In front of my children and my husband, I must be strong. I am the foundation of the family and I cannot crack," Katy explained.

Her solidity and strength paid off. Katy believes that her relationship with her husband has never been stronger. Bryan has fully recovered and gone back to school to become a physician assistant, even though he has no plans to retire from the military and will be deployed again in the fall. Dealing with his recovery has made their marriage more mature. She's not as naïve anymore about the dangers of deployment, but she also feels more prepared for their consequences.

"Acceptance is not giving up and letting the stress take over. It's about trusting that you will survive and thrive again."

Even if that healing acceptance is with you just for the day, somehow that makes everything okay.

* * *

Learning that a loved one has a TBI is a shocking and terrifying experience. The human brain is as delicate as it is important, and after injury it can be hard to predict what will happen. A TBI can mean breakdowns in verbal communication, coping with memory lapses, impaired vision, and other challenges. But as these two women have proven through their own grit and determination, a brain injury doesn't have to become an impassable roadblock in a marriage. Instead, it can become an unexpected gateway to closeness, understanding, and partnership.

CHAPTER 3

LIVING WITH IRON MAN: VISIBLE INJURIES COMPOUND THE SITUATION

You are so beautiful to me.
—JOE COCKER

"KNOW WHAT'S WORKED for me?" Julie said to a group of wives at SPA day. "Telling the kids their dad has become a Transformer."

The wives were swapping tips for helping their spouses and kids reconnect after the loss of a limb. TBI and PTS can be nearly invisible. Both cause stress and strife, forcing soldiers and their wives to create new lives around complex new disabilities. But many veterans return from war with far more visible injuries, including burns, scars, and amputated limbs. Coping with stares from strangers and unwelcome pity—not to mention the aggravation of learning to live with a disabled body—are just some of the challenges warriors and their wives must face. Recovery from a visible injury or amputation is a long, slow, and confusing process.

The Amputee Coalition of America describes six phases in the recovery process following amputation. In phase one, the amputee might make a conscious choice to focus on the present to get through the pain and block out distress about the future. In the second phase, the amputee experiences intense feelings of fear, denial, anger, depression, and confusion about the loss of their previous self. Phase three is about working to come to terms with the extent of the loss of limb or limbs and the loss's impact on the amputee's future. In phase four, the amputee begins to manage the recovery process by becoming aware of their strengths. In phase five, the focus is on creating new routines and finding priorities other than the loss. Not all amputees reach phase six, which involves becoming a mentally stronger person and confident role model by trusting oneself and others.

No matter which phase of recovery an amputee is in, he or she will struggle to understand and accept life with a devastating injury. And since so many American soldiers become injured in their early twenties, they face a lifetime with their wives and families during which the medical care they require may be costly, intensive, and constant. Amputees, for example, must be fitted for new prosthetics every few years. Eighty-three percent of veteran amputees have lost one or both legs, mostly from the blasts of IEDs, which means they must use wheelchairs or other aids to get around. These deadly homemade bombs are also the cause of most of the genital wounds that U.S. troops suffer, a class of injury that is painful and costly to treat.

Expensive as it may be, the financial cost of caring for a wounded warrior is dwarfed by the emotional cost. In some cases, wives are traumatized by watching their husbands lose limbs in the hospital after they've been rescued from combat, but they must adjust quickly and on the fly. And once they've finally left the hospital, these wives will remain emotionally and physically challenged in caring for and helping their military amputees adapt to a new life. When I work with couples in physical therapy, the wives sometimes pull me aside to tell me how they witness and experience their husband's phantom pain, and often feel as if they're living with the ghost of a life lost.

The wives report that one of the most effective ways to take care of themselves is through humor. I have enjoyed listening to their wry banter.

"For Halloween this year my husband took off his prosthetic and carried a fake bloody leg to our friends' Halloween party, and I went as a naughty nurse with a chain saw," said Fiona, a feisty brunette. "He's come so far from hiding in the house and refusing to go out because of the looks people give him. I loved seeing him be unashamed of his amputation at a party."

"If this can happen to my husband, what else can happen? When is the next foot going to fall off?" Jacqui quipped.

"Hey, my husband lost his leg after a bunch of failed operations, and the prosthetic works so much better than his damaged leg. He is our Iron Man now," Carla added.

Nothing is more rewarding to me than observing the strength of these women in meeting their challenges, and I know I am growing, too, as I help them heal themselves. The usual worries and complaints I hear from friends and family seem trivial now, compared to these ladies' challenges. I recognize how privileged I am in my own life—even when I face roadblocks—and I am learning more and more not to sweat the small stuff. I hope these stories change other lives as much as they have changed mine.

Let's meet Fiona, who stuck with her husband through phantom pain, suicidal thoughts, and more. His journey to recovery ended up changing her career path and igniting her passion for invention. Then we'll hear from Jacqui, who helped her injured husband relearn tasks that might seem impossible for someone who is missing limbs. Finally, Carla will share her story about the importance of open-mindedness and encourage us all to acknowledge and embrace the amputees in our own communities.

FIONA: MAKING LIFE WITHOUT LIMBS LIMITLESS

It was a routine, errand-filled day for Fiona when Patrick called from Afghanistan to tell her that he was heading out on an extensive mission and that she wouldn't hear from him for a few weeks. When the phone rang at 7:30 the next morning, she was caring for their four-month-old son, Stevie.

"I saw the call was foreign, but that it wasn't from Patrick, and I began to worry."

Her instincts were right. It was Marine headquarters, calling to say that Patrick had been injured and would be coming home. That was all the information they gave her.

"I was feeding little Stevie in my arms when I dropped to the ground," she recalled. "I was staying with my parents at the time, thank God, and my mother came running over to comfort me and help me understand what was going on. That date, July 4, 2012, is engraved on my heart."

Fiona couldn't stand not knowing what had happened or how badly Patrick had been hurt. She was so distraught, she threw up. Later that morning, Fiona received a call from Patrick confirming that he'd been injured and was on his way home.

"He didn't say much, only that both legs had been severely injured. He didn't have a lot of time to talk."

For eight long days, Fiona waited for Patrick to arrive back in the States, not knowing exactly when he would finally return. He would call at each stop, but he wasn't able to give her many details.

When Patrick finally told Fiona he had stepped on an IED, all she could think was, "Why him, God?" She was shocked to hear that all of his left leg and half his right foot had been blown off, but kept hoping she'd wake up from this horrible nightmare, that somehow it wasn't really true. She felt her world spinning out of control. Patrick had been a part of her life for so long. Would he still be the same man when he finally came home?

Fiona was a freshman and Patrick a junior when they met at a high school science fair. She was a studious, petite, blond science lover, and he a talkative Filipino baseball player. He watched, enthralled, as Fiona displayed her science project on biomechatronics. Theirs was an attraction of opposites, and they married right after high school in 2009. Thinking back on the early days of their relationship, Fiona said, "I found Patrick so handsome and charming." It didn't hurt that he was a romantic at heart, too. "He was always doing special things for me, like giving me sweet little gifts and leaving flowers on my car," she said, laughing. Her buff jock joined the Marines to serve his country, and she headed off to college to study biology and work as a yoga instructor.

During his time with the Marines, Patrick was deployed twice. Fiona found Patrick's second deployment to be the toughest, even before she received the call about his injuries. Patrick went to Afghanistan in April 2012 for active duty, while Fiona was home studying, working, and caring for their son. Fortunately, she was able to video chat with Patrick so that he could see Stevie grow.

"It was hard, though, when weeks would go by without talking to or seeing him," she said. "It made the days go by even more slowly."

Once Patrick returned to the States, Fiona found herself facing a whole new struggle, fighting and suffering alongside him as he endured numerous painful surgeries to get him to the point where his body could accommodate prosthetic legs. He underwent an amputation of his left leg and salvage interventions to save his lower right leg, battling infections throughout the ordeal.

"He was on so many medications for pain, he seemed like a different person. No emotion—not his normal funny and loving self," Fiona said. "Patrick was so strong through the whole process, keeping all of his emotions bottled up like the stoic

Marine he was trained to be. He had to bury the pain and 'suck it up' to carry on with the mission of healing, just as he had soldiered on through conflict in Afghanistan."

A year later, after many unsuccessful attempts to save his right leg, Patrick, Fiona, and a team of doctors came to the painful decision to amputate the leg just below the knee. The rehab process Patrick had been through for his left leg would have to start all over again.

"A double amputee! I didn't know if I could go through more surgeries and amputation while caring for little Stevie," Fiona recalled. "Some people call this the boomerang effect: just when you think everything is going smoothly, it comes back around and hits you hard. I felt like we were starting all over again. I was finally adjusting to caring for both my husband and our son while studying, and this setback was overwhelming."

At home after the second amputation, Patrick didn't want to go anywhere until swelling from the surgery went down and he could have prosthetics fitted. Then he could wear long pants and look "normal." The embarrassment of two stumps—one an amputation above the knee and the other below the knee—made him want to hide from the world.

He was also experiencing postamputation "phantom pain," often sensing that both legs were burning below the amputations. Imagine walking on your foot when it's asleep, or a charley horse that seems to last forever. Phantom pain is more excruciating than either, and it doesn't go away after a few minutes. The nerve endings at the site of the amputation continue to send pain signals to the brain, causing the brain to think the limb is still there. For some amputees, phantom pain lasts only a few months, but for Patrick it lasted more than a year. Doctors tried every drug available to diminish the pain, but under the influence of the painkillers, Patrick wasn't himself anymore. In fact, the medications brought him so low that he started thinking up a dozen ways to kill himself. He overmedicated himself, then turned to drinking to numb himself further. None of this helped his recovery process.

The physical wounds of war, everyone could see, but the mental wounds were the ones slowly killing him. Headlines from the war reinforced his feelings of guilt. The news showed Marines videotaping themselves while urinating on the bodies of dead Taliban soldiers, then posting the clips on YouTube; paratroopers staged macabre photos with the body parts of suicide bombers; an Army staff sergeant left his combat outpost in the middle of the night in southern Afghanistan to kill sixteen civilians, including nine children.

"This can't be our guys. We are the good ones," Fiona remembered Patrick saying.

Once he was able to scrub away the blood, dirt, and denial, and come to accept that he might have killed innocent people too, he didn't know how to live. How could he cross the bridge from conflict back to peacetime? How could he find meaning in his life as a wounded warrior? He needed to turn to someone, and Fiona was always there for him. She understood that it must be horrific for him to experience killing someone and almost be killed himself. She saw that the drugs, alcohol, and suicidal thoughts were his ways of avoiding the guilt and the fear of grief. Denial had been his coping mechanism until he finally opened up to Fiona, and she encouraged him to accept grief as a healthy response. He agreed to go to therapy at the VA. Grieving with a therapist required remembering the past, recalling difficult memories, and confronting the ugly truths of what he had seen, done, and failed to do in war.

Meanwhile, Fiona grappled with her own pain. She mourned the life they could have had if he were still healthy. The burly macho man who used to pick her up in his arms and swing her around now depended on her to hold *him* up, both physically and emotionally. Some days, Fiona doubted she could stay in the marriage. The peaks and valleys of the rehab process were not something she had ever anticipated. All the normal stuff of living took twice as long since she was helping Patrick shower, dress, wrap his stumps, and transfer from the wheelchair to the car. The endless appointments with doctors, physical therapists, and occupational therapists exhausted her.

Fiona struggled individually, but she and Patrick also struggled as a team. This couple, like many other wounded warriors and their wives, coped in the only way they knew how—they overbooked their lives. Every life task was done to excess: work, exercise, dieting, and occupational therapy. They hoped that if they moved fast enough and kept themselves busy enough, it would block out the anxiety, the flashbacks, and the night terrors. But soon the emotional distance and lack of intimacy between the couple was so deep, it was as if they no longer had any sort of connection. Hitting bottom, Fiona was brave enough to seek counseling to get the help she needed. And although it was taxing, she went to every medical appointment with Patrick, all while caring for their son and keeping up with her studies.

In the face of this staggering array of challenges, they both pushed on. Six months after his second amputation, Patrick began the journey of learning to walk with two prosthetic legs. He had gait-training appointments with a physical therapist three times a week. Fiona dropped in as often as she could to see his progress and meet with the prosthetist who had made and fitted his artificial legs.

While the physical therapist taught Patrick to walk on his new limbs, Fiona and the prosthetist worked on merging her man with machinery. Fiona was already scientifically inclined, and the biology, neuroscience, mechanics, electronics, and robotics involved in creating effective artificial limbs intrigued her. She wanted to learn more. Seeing Patrick light up as he learned to walk with his new legs inspired her. She decided to learn how to make devices that interact with human muscle and nervous systems, high-tech limbs that would give wounded warriors physical freedom again. She set out to get her master's degree in prosthetics. Never one to sit on the sidelines, she felt empowered to make a difference in not only her husband's life, but in the lives of other wounded warriors.

Miraculously, while Fiona focused on securing her degree in this growing field, she found herself falling in love with her husband all over again, watching him persevere and return to strength, becoming in some ways even stronger.

The couple also became friends with another wounded warrior amputee and his wife at the hospital during the therapy sessions. While the men were in physical therapy, the women chatted about their own trials and tribulations through the healing journey.

"Just take it one day at a time," Fiona's new friend advised her. "It's easy to look into the future and be afraid of what may happen. If things aren't going well with a fitting, you tend to hit a valley instead of a peak. You've got to take it day by day, because each day it will get better."

The first day Patrick walked on his own, he was filled with joy. Just that little bit of independence, that little bit of freedom, was enough to get him thinking, "Okay, I have a fighting chance." Today he tells others that, since that day, he hasn't "thought about suicide once, and self-medication is a thing of the past."

Fiona brought their son Stevie to therapy, and he called his dad "Superhero Transformer" when Patrick put on his "robot" leg. Impressing his son inspired Patrick even more as he learned to walk. They even joked about Stevie learning to run before his dad did, and the race to run was on!

Their new friends invited them to play with the Wounded Warrior Amputee Softball Team (WWAST). Patrick found new motivation playing with other active-duty and veterans who'd lost limbs in battle. He had the chance to travel the country playing able-bodied teams in competitive, celebrity, and exhibition games. Fiona loved the opportunity to travel and cheer him on. On and off the ball field, the family enjoyed spending time with other families who faced similar challenges.

The couple has also been empowering young boys and girls with missing limbs in the WWAST Kids Camp. Youngsters from all over the U.S. travel to the camp, which is run by veterans during their vacation time. The wives of the warrior amputees also get involved in playing and planning. Teaching young children with amputations and artificial limbs how to play games of softball brought the couple a sense of purpose and a common goal to help others. The camps are held in different cities each year.

"We all help each other. The kids help us, too," Fiona explained. She's happy that she and Patrick are giving back, not only to the kids they meet, but also to the kids that *these kids* will eventually help.

Over the next two years, Patrick earned his teaching degree and secured a job coaching baseball. He continued to make coaching at the kids' camp a priority, and playing with other wounded warriors is still a huge part of his life.

"The satisfaction of knowing that you have touched somebody's life and made them feel better about themselves, I mean, there's just nothing better," Patrick said, and Fiona agreed. At Fiona's graduation with a master's in prosthetics-orthotics, Patrick walked up to her on his new legs, one hand holding Stevie's and the other holding a bouquet of flowers with a card that read, "Congratulations! You've taught me—and will now teach others lying wounded in hospital beds—not to get down on themselves in spite of missing a limb. You've shown me that life without limbs can be limitless."

JACQUI: FROM TORN LIMBS TO FULL HEART

Jacqui has known her husband Alex since she was twelve years old. An all-American girl with optimism in spades and an Armenian boy with quiet curiosity, they grew up on the same street in Fresno, California. They had younger sisters who attended the same kindergarten and played together after school. Slowly they became friends in their adolescent years and, by the time they were teenagers, they became more than friends. They were the quintessential high school sweethearts, although they didn't get married until she was thirty years old and he was twenty-seven.

Jacqui knew there was a good chance that Alex would be sent overseas when he enlisted in the Army in 2004. She admired him for wanting to be part of something greater than himself, a warrior serving his country, and for taking advantage of this chance to travel and get a college education. He was following in his dad's footsteps to become an Army sergeant. But when he finally got the call, she felt mentally unprepared.

"I was very frightened when I first heard he was going to be deployed," Jacqui recalled, her big brown eyes tearing up as she relived the memory.

Both Jacqui and Alex grew up in military families, so they were familiar with the challenges and sacrifices that come with the life, but being with Alex before his deployment was more emotional than Jacqui had expected. She worked in admissions at a hospital emergency room and was accustomed to dealing with life-and-death situations. It was a challenge not to imagine Alex being in one.

Once Alex left for Iraq in 2006, Jacqui surrounded herself with family and friends in order to stay positive. She kept her mind busy by attending school full time, but she always made time to write her husband letters and emails. Sometimes they even got to speak on the phone.

Driving home from school one afternoon, Jacqui received a call that nearly caused her to crash the car. Alex had been injured and would be returning home early. She was informed that she could see him at Walter Reed Army Medical Center, and she immediately flew to Washington, DC, to be by his side. Her mind raced as she considered the possibilities. How bad were his injuries? What would he look like? Would she even recognize her husband?

"I walked down the hallway to his room. It was late at night, and I didn't know what to expect," she said. "I broke down and started crying just a few doors away from his room."

Jacqui summoned the courage to continue down the hallway. She pushed her short brown hair behind an ear and forced herself to put one foot in front of the other. When she arrived at Alex's door, he was sitting up watching TV with a big smile on his face.

"Hi, baby," he said.

It was a *huge* relief to be able to look at him, recognize him, and know the man she'd married was back. But they were hardly out of the woods. Alex had multiple surgical procedures ahead of him.

While he had been out on patrol, an enemy combatant had detonated an IED directly under his Humvee, just as he was crossing a bridge. Alex was facing the rear in the gunner's hatch when the IED went off. The explosion shredded his right arm, and massive amounts of shrapnel embedded themselves in his right leg, causing deep-tissue wounds. Alex's right arm had to be amputated above the elbow, and he was diagnosed with PTS. This was just the beginning of a difficult physical and psychological journey.

He stayed at Walter Reed Army Medical Center for an entire year. He was right-handed, and it took months of physical and occupational therapy for him to learn to use his left hand for everything he needed to do. Suddenly the simplest of things, such as writing or holding a spoon, became enormous challenges.

"I had to help him with brushing his teeth, combing his hair, and shaving," Jacqui said. "It was so surreal."

His rehabilitation was further complicated by the injuries to his leg. He was in an extraordinary amount of pain, pain that persists to this day. He was also losing a lot of weight.

"Things were really difficult in the beginning. Not only did he have to learn how to do everything with his left hand, we knew nothing about PTS." Alex was an independent man, and became frustrated when he couldn't do everything by himself. He needed help, even if he didn't know how to ask for it. Jacqui was with him every step of the way, and the sacrifices she made had a profound impact on her life. She became his only support system, leaving her job in California to stay permanently in Washington, DC, far from both of their families.

Jacqui knew from the get-go that in order to help Alex, she would need a lot of help herself. So she was incredibly relieved when they were introduced to a counselor through the Wounded Warrior Project immediately following Alex's amputation. Representatives from the organization walked them through the steps of Alex's recovery and reentry into the civilian world. The counselor met with them weekly to help with the mounds of paperwork, and connected them with families who had gone through the transition before them. Facing down the loss of Alex's arm and other medical complications, they both felt scared. The other families told them what to expect, reminding them that there would be many struggles now and down the road. Jacqui found the assistance invaluable.

"It helped our marriage become what it is today," she said. "We have many friends within the Wounded Warrior Project that we are very close to and consider family."

Knowing more resources were available to her, Jacqui didn't stop there. A social media expert and connection-making powerhouse, she dug into research to see what she could find. Through the VA, she got in touch with another caregiver,

Alisa, whose husband's injuries were similar to Alex's. Meeting someone whose challenges were similar to her own was such a relief, and it helped her feel grounded. Through Alisa's assistance, Jacqui cultivated a better understanding of how to help her husband as both a caregiver and a spouse.

For instance, Jacqui would grow frustrated when Alex insisted on doing everything for himself. Alisa had gone through the same cycle with her own husband and shared her insight: Jacqui wasn't recognizing that in spite of his extensive injuries, it was very difficult for Alex to accept a helping hand. Sharing and discussing helped Jacqui understand that this was a natural part of the healing process.

"Alisa had gone through much of what I was going through," Jacqui said of her new friend. "I learned there was a difference between what Alex needed and what *I felt* I needed to do for him."

As it turned out, Alex's physical rehabilitation was only half the journey. Although his amputation was quite visible, it took years for them both to learn the hidden signs and symptoms of PTS. Alex suffered through nightmares of seeing his best buddy die. He asked himself again and again, as he replayed the scene in his mind, if he could have done more to save him. He slowly opened up to Jacqui to tell her how his tour experience varied from extreme boredom to extreme chaos. He told her that boredom could be worse than battle, and that often the men were itching to break the tedium. Nervousness, grief, rage, and terror need outlets, and many of his fellow soldiers felt that the only means of release was a gun. Attempting to explain how he'd been affected by the death of his best friend, John, he described his nightmares—including this one, which he wrote down in 2010, years after the blast:

> I ask John does he want a glass of water. He nods and smiles. I say I'll be right back. He nods and smiles again. I take a step. I hear a blast. A bullet is crashing into John's face. It is blowing apart. I hit the ground as

he does. I grab my rifle. I want to kill. I have to. I crawl
to John. I put my hands on him. I try to stop the blood.
There is nothing I can do. Nothing.

This nightmare and others haunted Alex. Over time, Jacqui
learned that certain events would make Alex feel as if he were no
longer in control of his anger. For example, large crowds often
made him feel uncomfortable. Something as simple as a pizza
box on the side of the road would trigger memories of the IED,
and he would maneuver the car to the farthest lane possible. It
surprised her to see how many simple things set him off. An even
bigger surprise was learning that Jacqui felt acute stress herself,
caused by the helplessness she experienced while watching her
husband suffer.

But they worked together and, along with their friends from
the Wounded Warrior Project, they began to understand and cope
with the roller coaster of living with the condition. Throughout
that wild ride, Jacqui continued to educate and empower herself
by taking classes and seminars offered by the VA. Not only did
these educational offerings allow her to connect with others in
her situation, they also enabled her to share her story and hear
about the recovery experiences of other wounded warriors back
home. She is currently working toward her bachelor of science
in public administration, public policy, and leadership, with the
goal of working for a nonprofit organization that helps veterans
and their caregivers.

"I hope to work on the mental health side of things," Jacqui
said. "My husband has been a huge support for me in pursuing
my goals. He has been my rock, as I continue to be his."

Alex is also a student and is currently enrolled in online
graduate school at the University of Southern California, where
he's pursuing a master's degree in social work. Alex feels that his
next mission as a warrior is to help younger warriors transition
to life at home.

"We both have dreams of working with the VA and helping our veterans and caregivers in any way possible," Jacqui said. "With all we have been through, I am sure we can help others."

Alex also enjoys scuba diving and surfing, never letting his injuries hold him back from doing the things he loves. Prior to his injury, Alex had been an avid guitar player. Jacqui was afraid that if he lost his ability to play—an activity that had always given him peace and satisfaction—he might become disheartened and depressed. But she needn't have worried; one thing that remained unchanged about Alex's personality was his inability to take "no" for an answer. Whenever he was presented with an obstacle, he pushed himself to overcome it. The more that people told him he couldn't do something, the more he wanted to prove them wrong. The military had taught him to be disciplined, goal oriented, and strong. He used these skills to push through his recovery and relearn the tasks that were important to him.

Alex taught himself to use his right "hook" as a pick while his uninjured left hand created the chords. Music became their therapy, helping them both heal from the wounds of war. Alex describes the horrors he saw in war as giving him soul sickness. Jacqui helps him write songs that grapple with such questions as, "Did I commit murder?" "Have I done good or evil?" and "If I've done evil, then what am I?" Morality themes are pervasive in his songs. During his tour in Iraq, it was either kill or be killed; there was no time to think. It wasn't until after he'd recovered from his physical injuries that he really began to think about the moral issues inherent in being a soldier.

Alex told Jacqui that "If we don't address the moral issues, we can't recover from the PTS, no matter how much medication or therapy we are given." They discussed whether it was even possible to serve in a war that was *not* immoral, that did not cause the soul inner conflict, and from which soldiers could emerge clean.

Watching Alex overcome obstacles on his journey helped Jacqui become a better caregiver and a stronger spouse. Part of the struggle was learning the difference—the roles overlapped but were also distinct. Jacqui learned there were times when she needed to step back and give Alex his space, but still make sure he knew she was there for him. It's a balancing act that they strive to maintain each and every day.

"My advice for anyone who experiences a tragedy like this is to hold on to the person you know and love," Jacqui said. "Along the way you may get a little lost, but that's okay. You'll find your way back to each other *through* each other."

CARLA: UNINVITED, UNWELCOME, UNFRIENDED

Carla couldn't even remember the last time Alan actually *wanted* to get out on a Saturday night. But a week before Christmas he certainly seemed to, and totally without nudging. There was no tense waiting for the "right" moment, or the awkward silence that loomed after a blowout altercation. There was no shaming, name-calling, or complaints about how she "didn't understand." There was just a husband who appeared to be showing signs of excitement. It was quite possibly a Christmas miracle in the making.

It was the first "normal" event the couple had been invited to since Alan's return from his most recent deployment to Iraq more than a year earlier. Carla—a petite, gregarious Latina hairstylist in her early thirties—was beginning to believe people only thought of the two of them on Veterans Day and the Fourth of July. Even then, there were no invites to parties, only polite texts and hat tips.

But the very day that the Christmas party invitation arrived, Carla allowed herself the indulgence of imagining her party outfit possibilities. And while her hopes were up, they certainly weren't sky-high as she placed the invitation discreetly between the salt- and pepper shakers on the dinner table, right where she knew Alan would find it.

When she walked into the living room the following day and found the invitation relocated to the coffee table, she knew to keep quiet. Alan would address it in his own time. She had prepared for an exhausting bargaining session, but was instead caught off guard by Alan wheeling his now-slight frame past her down the hallway with a casual, "You wanna check out Bill and Tish's Christmas party?"

She nearly fainted from excitement and disbelief, but knew better than to reveal her desperation to get out of the house. Instead, she returned the casual inquiry with a simple, "I'm in." Counselors say to "capture" the good days, and Carla fully intended to do just that. She couldn't help but think that this Christmas party was more than just a holiday function for her and Alan; it was the first step toward a new territory of socializing for them both, but for Alan especially. This was their chance to not only prove that they could still have fun and make great memories despite their circumstances, but also to hush all the "Oh, what a shame" sympathizers. Carla longed for the day that she could exchange *pleasantries* with people, instead of absorbing their pity. She crossed her fingers for the next three weeks, praying Alan wouldn't change his mind . . . or mood.

Just in case, Carla made sure her party outfit was pressed and ready to dazzle. Alan suggested wearing a Santa suit to hide the scars from his burns, which covered 40 percent of his body. She was touched that his humor seemed to be peeking through, and knew he was looking for a way to make everyone else comfortable. His selflessness tugged at her heartstrings.

The week of the party arrived, and Carla was making the grocery list for her hit holiday recipe—coffee-flavored tarts— when her cell phone rang. She flipped back her thick black hair and pressed the phone to her ear, glad to hear her friend's voice. She also wanted to ask Tish about the parking arrangements on Alan's behalf, so the timing worked out perfectly.

"Hi, Tish, I bet you're a busy woman today," Carla said playfully, while she busily finished up the grocery list.

"Well, Carla, I'm afraid I've got a bit of an uncomfortable request for you." Tish's voice sounded hesitant.

Carla set her pen down and took a seat at the table. Her gut told her she would need to be seated for this, whatever it was.

"You know we love you and Alan with all our hearts, and we'd love nothing more than to celebrate the season with you," Tish began. "But the thing is, we're going to have two other families at the party who have fathers in the service. Both have small children that will be in tow. One of the mothers is worried that if her children see Alan, they'll assume what happened to him can happen to their dad as well."

Tish paused, and Carla braced herself for what was coming next.

"The other gal coming has a husband who is about to deploy, and we've heard she's having a real hard time with it. Seeing Alan could be difficult for her and the kids, too. I really hate asking you to sit this one out, but I'm just trying to do what's best for everybody. Maybe we can swing by after church on Sunday and do some Christmas visiting then?"

Carla was shocked and completely speechless. She didn't feel like she and Alan were being uninvited from a party. She felt like they were being unfriended, period. Apparently Tish picked up on this from Carla's lack of response and quickly added, "It was my mistake. I sent the invites out from our Christmas-card list and didn't think of this beforehand. I'm so sorry. I hope you understand."

And that she did. Carla understood a lot of things in that very moment. She understood how Alan must have felt on a daily basis when people selected the next line at the store (even though at the moment it might be longer) just so they wouldn't have to stand behind him, or avoided eye contact even in the hospital hallways. She understood how it must feel to watch the same people who fly American flags off their porches and gather canned goods "for the troops" shun him in person, turning away from his burn marks and the shrunken figure. But mostly she understood that everything had changed. Alan had changed, and even when he tried to reconnect with the man he used to be, there were roadblocks keeping him trapped in his "new" form.

Carla knew that *she* had changed, too. She no longer wanted to dress up and go out, to put on makeup for the first time in months and wear her silky cream blouse and red earrings. She wanted Christmas to be over. She wanted all of it to just be over.

The truth was, Alan and Carla had been married for less than a year when, on his return from Iraq in 2010, he was thrust into the unanticipated role of "wounded soldier," and her newlywed glow became the perspiration of "caregiver."

The first hours of their "new life" were nothing short of traumatic whiplash. On one hand, Carla was eternally grateful to have her partner back alive. She knew that many wounded soldiers return home in vegetative states or in need of amputations. While severe burns covered almost half of Alan's body, marring his olive skin and eradicating most of his dark, wiry hair, at least she didn't have those choices to make.

The year following his injuries was a constant dance of conflict, misunderstanding, and negotiation. Carla would unintentionally push his buttons when she'd prod him to be more active. In turn, he'd accuse her of trying to run his life. When she blamed his drugs for his aggressive behavior, he tried to wean himself off them and became sick. Fights became more frequent. At one point, he grabbed a gun and locked himself in the bedroom for several tension-filled hours. He emerged hours later saying he wanted to commit suicide, almost as if he were making an announcement and asking her permission at the same time. She was so empty by that point that she told him the decision was up to him, but she wasn't going to support it or help him do it. He began crying, and they found themselves in the familiar "sob and hold."

She became fearful of his suicide attempts and would rummage through his drawers and secret hiding spots for suicide notes. About a year and a half after he'd been injured, she found his journal.

She knew it was wrong and invasive to read his private thoughts, but she also knew she had to find a way to connect to what was inside his head, holding him hostage. She opened the journal to the first page and found he had jumped right in. His handwriting scribbled in an old notebook was hard to read:

Nothing prepares you for killing, and seeing your best friends die. I had to choose the "lesser of the two evils" on a daily basis, "kill or be killed."

Nothing prepares you for seeing such destruction and devastation. I saw bombed-out houses and homeless Iraqis who lived in mud huts and watched children play and drink water from dirty puddles. In one incident that haunts me, I watched a screaming wounded woman beg us for medical help. Our convoy just passed her by, citing orders not to stop. We didn't know who was who. We felt like we were fighting ghosts. We didn't know where the enemy was. There were jihadists with bombs hiding all around us. I can't forget that woman. I looked that woman in her eyes and saw her humanity, but I kept going.

How do you recover from this?

Carla passed a weary hand over her face and placed the journal back into the bottom of his nightstand drawer beneath the stacks of medical pamphlets. As she left the room, she realized she now possessed the awareness she needed to understand Alan. She had uncovered the "secret" token of knowledge that most wives of the wounded spend lifetimes trying to find. She couldn't have predicted that exposing herself to his memories would mean that now his truth haunted two people.

Carla couldn't let any more time go by without seeking outside help. She signed herself and Alan up for FOCUS Family Resilience Training, a program offered to military families to help them overcome challenges. They found a counselor who helped them both become stronger to adapt to their new life together. The training left them feeling more prepared for the little crises and obstacles that seemed to pop up unexpectedly, and this was a huge help. But as the couple cleared one hurdle, another presented itself.

"FOCUS helped, but it didn't solve all our problems," Carla told the ladies at SPA Day. "I still felt frustrated and stressed, and Alan still faced so many physical challenges. The bathroom incident is a classic example."

She had left the house to run an errand, only to come back and find Alan stranded in the bathroom. He'd had to use the toilet and had gotten in okay, but couldn't get back into his chair because it wouldn't fit between the sink and the toilet. He'd been stranded on the toilet for three hours waiting for her to come home.

The incident lit a fire under Carla, who became determined to make their home a safe and navigable place for her husband. She tapped into her "Erin Brokovich" willpower and began researching, finding out what it would take to make their house a wheelchair-accessible home. Such renovations are costly, and they're still making a few changes, but by installing ramps, support bars, and other helpful features, Carla has made Alan's home life considerably easier.

A little more than five years after the IED blast that shattered their lives, Alan and Carla have reached a better place. Carla found part-time work as a hairstylist at a fabulous local salon, and getting back to work renewed her passion. Alan found work as a hiring manager for an IT firm, where he analyzes resumes and compiles the top candidates for the HR department. It's not his dream job, but the sense of "doing" has helped him feel productive and grounded, that he's contributing to the family's stability. While he still uses a wheelchair, his pain is easing and his emotions are more stable.

As for Carla, she's enjoying moving on from being a caregiver and embraces her own identity as a hairstylist. She knew she had to stop being Alan's wife *and* his mother, but it was hard for both of them to let go of those roles. She felt anxious and guilty when she stopped attending his appointments, but she pushed through, knowing that it was time to relinquish those duties. She never imagined being a military wife would be so life-changing, but she doesn't regret marrying Alan. Not for one minute. Her marriage has shaped her life's journey, made her stronger, and showed her just how resilient she can be.

She sympathizes with other wives of wounded warriors who are still mired in the stress and struggle of adjusting to life with a disabled husband. She remembers the mounting pressure of having to hold the family together through painful hospital stays, flashbacks, complex paperwork, and therapy.

One important step Carla took to make her life with Alan more manageable was to attend an Operation Homefront Hearts of Valor retreat. Hearts of Valor recognizes that what the wives of wounded warriors need most is support, encouragement, and time to focus on themselves—all which can seem out of reach if they're left to cope all alone. The retreats are designed specifically for service caregivers with those exact objectives in mind. Imagine a room full of caregivers finally able to connect with each other, trade tips on how to handle the logistics of managing a home, and enjoy solo time to recharge. Many of the women who attend Hearts of Valor retreats are fresh-faced twenty- or thirty-year-olds who have little experience with difficult, life-altering situations. They sometimes appear speechless, stunned into silence by their new, overwhelming lives. More seasoned caregivers often break down in relief when they realize they've finally found a community that actually *does* understand them.

At the retreat Carla attended, each caregiver got to chart her emotions before and after a few days of time on their own. When they arrived at the retreat, caregivers said they felt "worried," "tired," and "overwhelmed." By the time they headed home, their words had changed to "relaxed," "motivated," "refreshed," and "excited."

Carla found her experience so rejuvenating that she now volunteers at retreats, passing along her newfound strength to other wives. She recognizes that service to our country isn't just limited to lacing up a pair of combat boots. And when people in her life express a desire to help, she urges them to contact Hearts of Valor to see how they can be of service.

With the memory of being disinvited from the Christmas party still lingering in her mind, she has become more vocal about the importance of including wounded warriors in celebrations. Our culture tends to get lazy when it comes to expressing gratitude toward the brave men and women who have fought to defend our nation. We figure that the military itself will do the heavy lifting, providing formal honors, financial support, and medical care, while the rest of us turn away. They deserve to be seen, to be thanked, to be included. They are the one percent of the population that is sent into battle to do the dirty work.

Now that you have heard her story, Carla hopes that the next time you plan a social gathering, you'll think of inviting the guy in the wheelchair next door. That simple, easy gesture will go a long way toward making a wounded warrior feel visible, important, and valued.

* * *

When you see a wheelchair, think "Iron Man." When you see a prosthetic limb, think "Transformer." Because that's what these warriors truly are. People talk about being willing to risk "life and limb" for causes or people, and they cast the phrase about casually. But these brave men and women have risked their lives and lost their limbs in order to protect our freedom. And their wives have so much to teach us all about adapting to change, resiliency, and overcoming hurdles.

CHAPTER 4

A REASON TO LIVE: THE SUICIDE EPIDEMIC

He who has a why to live can bear almost any how.
—FRIEDRICH NIETZSCHE

AFTER THE SHOCK and sadness of witnessing the veteran's suicide on the Coronado Bridge that May 2015 day, I reached out to counselors at the VA for information that I could use to educate myself and share with families who suspect their wounded warriors might be thinking of suicide. They provided me with many tools and insights, which I share as often as I can. The more readily people are able to recognize the signs of a suicidal mind-set, the better our chances of making those alarming suicide numbers tick downward.

Here are six important things to know and do if someone in your life seems at risk for suicide:

1. People who commit suicide don't want to die; they just want to quit hurting.

Typically, the goal of the person considering suicide is to find a way to stop the pain they are experiencing, as well as the pain they are causing others. One thing I've learned as a physical therapist is we can never truly know another person's pain, and everyone we come into contact with has experienced pain in some form or another. Many times, people who are suffering feel as though no one understands what they are going through. If you know someone who appears deeply depressed, offer to listen and ask if there's anything you can do to help lessen their pain.

2. If a friend says he or she wants to die, take it seriously.

People who commit suicide usually think about it for a long period of time before they act on their urges. Sometimes they drop hints and leave clues, or even tell people what they are planning, in order to "see if anyone cares." Always take these threats seriously. Dismissing a suicidal threat feeds into the person's belief that people don't care or won't miss them when they're gone. Every threat is serious. Many people express their intentions in the hopes that someone will take notice or talk them out of it. Be that person. Never miss an opportunity to give someone hope.

3. Get professional help.

If someone you know is suffering and considering suicide, encourage them to call the National Suicide Prevention Lifeline at 1-800-273-TALK (8255). Trained counselors are always there, ready to help. They know what to say, they know how to listen, and they've heard it all before. If that someone is you—call today! Additional resources are listed at the end of this book.

4. Be proactive.

Consistent, short-term support is key in dealing with someone who is contemplating suicide. Oftentimes, suicidal urges are compounded by a depressed state of mind. Just because someone reached out to you once doesn't mean they'll do so again. They might feel guilty for having burdened you with their pain and will avoid contacting you again. Don't wait for them to come to you; reach out and check in often. Let them know you're there for them by calling them on the phone and offering to spend time with them.

5. Encourage positive lifestyle changes.

Quite often, suicidal urges are experienced and expressed during times of chaos and confusion, such as periods of high stress, intense depression, or chronic alcohol and drug abuse. Do what you can to eliminate these stressors and encourage healthy behaviors, such as getting exercise, eating well, and getting enough rest at night. Something as simple as a walk with a friend or coffee with a loved one can promote physical and emotional health.

6. Make a safety plan.

Suicidal thoughts don't necessarily lead to suicide— but once they appear, they tend to stick around. They linger as a possibility, a way out, a means to an end. Identify trigger points, such as the anniversary of an injury or the death of a fellow warrior. Monitor changes in use of drugs or alcohol. Be on the lookout for the calm before the storm. A wounded warrior's wife or caregiver needs to be aware that positive changes in her warrior's demeanor—such as appearing suddenly calmer and more elevated in mood—can sometimes result from a decision to commit suicide at some future time.

* * *

In my work, I have learned that suicide casts a long shadow on the lives it touches. In several instances, children of veterans who have threatened or attempted suicide—including children as young as thirteen—have themselves later threatened or attempted suicide. A veteran's suicidal statements can spill over to his children, conveying the message that life is not worth living. They reason, "My dad is big and stronger than me, a warrior even. If he cannot handle life, how can I ever hope to do so?"

I've seen some veterans with suicidal thoughts attempt to avoid the stigma of suicide by engaging in reckless behavior with automobiles and motorcycles, or by placing themselves in dangerous situations where they invite other people to attack. Among some veterans, there might also be a mind-set that violence—even violence against one's self—is a viable solution to life's problems. Risky behavior is a way to get killed.

Some wives incarcerated for the murder or attempted murder of their veteran spouses after suffering domestic violence have described their husbands as "begging to die." In one instance, a veteran suffering from PTS beat his wife to the point where she needed hospitalization, then handed her a pistol and dared her to shoot him.

"I've seen plenty of death in Afghanistan," he said. "I'm not afraid to die."

Soldiers' time in war often gives them the impression that violence is a justifiable method of problem solving. When they are on duty, the answers to many problems are often violent. These veterans have seen death and may have killed others, including noncombatants.

None of this is easy to handle, and we must do the best we can to offer support where it is needed. This extends to the families of those who have completed suicides. When I meet the wives of wounded warriors whose husbands, brothers, or fathers have taken their own lives, they speak about the guilt they carry, feeling that they could have done something to stop these men. They share their feelings of shame in our support group. They are embarrassed to have someone in the family who killed themselves. How can their children go to school and tell their classmates? These children are often angry with their fathers for committing suicide and think, "How could he abandon me? How could he let me see him die?"

So, what is the silver lining around this dark cloud? Some women find new meaning in their lives after their warriors have committed suicide. They channel their grief into helping others. These are remarkable women who discover a new inner resilience in the aftermath of the trauma. Many become active in suicide prevention organizations, helping veterans and those still on active duty to see the signs and find help before they consciously or subconsciously make the decision to end their lives.

These stories give me strength when I need it. Because I live in Coronado, I regularly cross the bridge where I saw how easily a wounded warrior can step to the edge and end his life in a blink of an eye. Every time the memory comes back to me, I reflect on what I can do to ease the suffering of those around me.

The following stories are from Suzie, Sheila, and Lexi, who generously share the insights they've gained. All three women explain how they and their wounded warriors found meaning in their lives after a suicide attempt.

SUZIE: UNCONQUERED

When Suzie walked into the hospital room, her new patient was lying on his bed with the covers pulled over his head. She paused, wondering if her patient was traumatized or playing a game. When he peeked out of the covers, she saw a twinkle in his eyes that let her know that despite his severe injuries, he was full of mischief.

The petite, brown-eyed physical therapist with the bubbly personality and gentle touch made an immediate impression on Sam, too. He perked up when she came to visit him twice a day to perform range-of-motion exercises on his limbs.

Sam wasn't like Suzie's other patients. He'd made twenty deployments in fifteen years in special operations. His run of good luck ended in Fallujah in 2007, where a shot in the back left him paraplegic. He had a long road ahead of him as he adjusted to his new life without the use of his legs.

Sam had been a sniper, an elite athlete, and mentally tough. From their first appointment together, Suzie believed this strong-minded warrior had what it took to thrive. She taught him how to transfer from his bed to his wheelchair, then from the chair to a car. He eventually learned how to use his wheelchair so he could go up ramps and over curbs and get around town. He even learned how to drive a car using hand controls. After six months of rehab, he left the hospital in his wheelchair, an independent forty-year-old man.

After Sam was discharged in 2008, he often visited Suzie in the rehab center to watch her work with patients he'd bonded with during his own therapy. They started dating and were engaged within a year. Two years after they met, they were married in her hometown in England before returning to live in the United States.

Suzie looked forward to their life together. Since he had already overcome so many daunting challenges, she didn't know a new struggle was just beginning for Sam. Despite appearances, he had a hard time adjusting to civilian life. One day he was fine, and the next he would burrow so deeply inward that Suzie wondered if he'd ever resurface.

"Our marriage was not what I imagined," she said. "Since he was physically independent, I thought the emotional adjustment would be easy, but that was the hardest part."

Sam was often withdrawn, angered easily, suffered from frequent nightmares, and hated being in crowded places. He would either act out aggressively or avoid contact with people altogether. He refused to form emotional bonds with people he didn't know, and he didn't trust anyone, including his new bride. However, there was another, softer side to Sam. He was a great helper and often did all he could for her. Suzie was confused by these conflicting personas.

"His mood swings had me waking up every morning wondering what version of him I would see that day," she explained.

As a sniper deployed to Iraq, Sam had been exposed to tragic deaths and horrifically traumatic events. He told Suzie that, from a psychological point of view, he was barely holding it together when he was shot. For a while, losing use of his legs had trumped his psychological issues, but those issues had come back full force.

Suzie knew that if he was going to be truly rehabilitated, he would need to work through the trauma of his war memories. One of the most frustrating aspects of this new situation was that Suzie felt unable to make things right for Sam, to fix him. That was her job, after all: to rehabilitate people. But she was too close to Sam to be his guide. She acknowledged that if Sam was going to move on and deal with his emotional issues, he needed a specialist. Suzie was determined to help Sam find a therapist through the VA system, but this became a challenge for several reasons, the number one reason being Sam himself.

"Some were unlucky enough to die over there, some unlucky to be injured, and some unlucky to suffer from PTS," Sam said. "I knew in my head I was lucky to come home alive, but survivor's guilt is strong. The hardest part for a man's man like me would be sticking with the therapy."

Initially, Sam took the medications as prescribed and went to therapy, but after a few months he thought he was "man enough" to go it alone. At the mercy of his bravado, the PTS was pushed below the surface. Although some ups and downs continued, their life together more or less stabilized, and they welcomed their first child in January 2010. Suzie was elated to be a mother, and Sam was a wonderfully hands-on father.

Sam's mood swings, however, continued. He overreacted to things that weren't a big deal, and when something actually *was* a big deal, he acted as if it weren't. He took the concept of "road rage" to a new level, throwing curse-laden temper tantrums whenever someone cut him off or honked at him, beating the steering wheel with his hands. But when the baby came down with a high fever and had to be rushed to urgent care, he was stony-faced and silent, leaving Suzie to feel panicky and abandoned. After pursuing Suzie so vigorously, he went back and forth about wanting to be married and would sometimes threaten divorce. To outsiders, they looked like a happy family, so much so that friends and family found it hard to understand the depth of Sam's turmoil and the range of ways his PTS would manifest itself.

"You would never know there was anything wrong with him," Suzie said, "and that's what makes invisible illnesses like PTS so tricky. No one in my family understood what I was going through with him."

As Sam's condition worsened, so did his ability to handle his own emotions. As is often the case with those who refuse to take prescribed drugs, he sought other means of relieving the pain and suffering, layering substance abuse onto an already complicated issue.

While he was sinking into the depths, though, Sam began to process what had happened to him and share his experiences with Suzie. He talked about participating in things he didn't understand and that were hard to describe. He was haunted by the murders of innocent children that he had witnessed. He confessed that war had changed him and robbed him of any innocence he might have had. He told Suzie that he felt as if his body was no better than a cage, a source of problems and pain. He was dealing with severe spasticity in his legs and endurance issues due to his lowered respiratory capacity. Though paralyzed, he insisted his injuries caused pain that not even the strongest medicines could dull. He complained of "a screaming agony in every nerve ending in my body."

Suzie watched helplessly as his depression deepened. He was falling into a pit, and it became harder and harder to pull him out. He no longer kept his substance abuse from her as he became resigned to a lifetime of purposelessness and pain.

"My life mattered when I was with my team fighting for my country," he told her, "but now, in a wheelchair, I feel like a burden. I've tried to deal with it on my own so that you could feel like I was still here for you. But, really, I feel like a prop, just taking up space instead of helping."

Suzie knew Sam was telling her he was giving up, and she could feel her husband slipping away. In early 2011, four years after his injury, suicide began to seem like a viable option to Sam. He felt obligated to hang on for his family's sake, but he was losing faith in his ability to do so.

By this time, his mind had become a wasteland filled with visions of incredible horror, unceasing depression, and crippling anxiety—even with all of the medications the doctors gave him. Simple things that everyone else took for granted were nearly impossible for him. He couldn't laugh or cry, couldn't feel anything anymore. He believed his experiences in Iraq had taken everything away from him. He was too crippled to be at war, too damaged to be at peace. When he thought about ending it all, he didn't see it as suicide, but as a mercy killing. He knew about killing. He knew how to end it all quickly and painlessly. He believed his death would free him from pain and suffering, and he also believed that Suzie and their son would no longer be burdened with him.

Sam outlined his plans in a letter he left for Suzie to find: he was going to go to a nearby bridge and jump. In a panic, she called 911 and the operator instructed her to make contact with him so the police could find him. She called Sam and begged him to meet her somewhere before he went to the bridge. She was able to convince him to see her, and after she'd calmed him down a bit, the police arrived and took him to a hospital.

But that wasn't the end of his battle. Sam spent the next year and a half fighting off thoughts of suicide, and his struggle exhausted them both. There were days, Suzie was convinced, that the only thing stopping Sam from ending it all was a lack of energy. He certainly had the desire.

Suzie knew it was only a matter of time before Sam succeeded in his suicide plan, so in 2013 she reached out to the VA again, and again she found the system difficult to navigate. Eventually her husband's new case manager placed Sam with a psychologist who was very skilled and truly cared about his patients. That made all the difference in the world.

Under this psychologist's guidance, Suzie committed herself to learning everything she could about her husband's illness. She attended weekly sessions with a VA counselor to find out more about PTS. After much information gathering, she finally understood why Sam couldn't go to the fair with the family or to Disneyland with his son. It wasn't the wheelchair, but the hypervigilance that exhausted him. It was impossible for Sam to enjoy himself when he was on high alert. He had been in an environment where anyone or anything could be a threat—passersby, the ground at his feet, even children—and hypervigilance became a matter of survival. In many ways, Sam was still in the desert, stuck in that terrible place.

During the therapeutic process, they both learned more about suicidal ideation. Sam learned that, just as with physical pain, everyone has his or her emotional limit. Together, they began to understand why he was feeling what he was feeling, why he couldn't recognize that he had options or believe things would ever get better. They took solace in the fact that they could fight these feelings together.

The therapist gave them many tools, including affirmations that Sam wasn't alone in this struggle, that he was loved by many people. Suzie reminded herself that Sam didn't really want to die, but strove to kill the pain that kept him from the life he was capable of living. She learned to accept that while she couldn't give Sam a reason to live, with compassion and understanding she could help him search for a reason within himself.

Having worked with patients of failed suicide attempts as a physical therapist, Suzie was a believer in the power of love. She also knew that if caregivers focused too much attention on their spouses, other family members could grow resentful. When Sam acted out, she reminded her son that it had nothing to do with him.

"We didn't make this happen to your dad, and we can't fix it for him," she repeated again and again to her little boy.

While Sam attended his counseling appointments and group therapy, Suzie concentrated on keeping both herself and her son healthy. She realized that she had no control over whether her husband would learn to trust others, be comfortable in crowded places, and not overreact to petty things. But she could control how she reacted to him.

Suzie started to work on her own health and feelings of worthiness by pursuing her career goals and raising her son. She let Sam find his path to recovery without pressuring him with her judgment or unrealistic expectations. She practiced compassion and understanding instead of seeking quick fixes to problems. When Sam tried to discourage her from leaving him to attend an appointment with her therapist, she reminded Sam that she loved him but she needed to do this for herself.

With determination and ongoing support, Sam learned how to cope with the nightmares, depression, and flashbacks. It was a long, slow road, but he stuck to it. The combination of a skilled therapist, a newfound understanding of his condition, and a supportive wife worked wonders on his healing process. He no longer felt that his life was meaningless and empty, and he devoted himself wholeheartedly to raising his son. He even returned to school in 2015 to obtain a master's degree in computer science. He found a new career working for the military on a contract basis and, through group therapy, learned about the Invictus Games, which opened a new chapter in his life.

The international Invictus Games offer Paralympics-style sporting events in which injured veterans can compete. Events include wheelchair basketball, sitting volleyball, and indoor rowing. Invictus is Latin for "unconquered" or "invincible." The first Invictus Games were inspired by the Warrior Games in the United States and took place in 2014 at Queen Elizabeth Olympic Park in London. Sam threw himself into the games, and soon the competitive juices that had flowed through him during his long military career began to flow again. At this writing, he is training to compete in the 2016 Invictus Games in Orlando, Florida.

Suzie loves going to the games to cheer Sam on, to see friends, and to celebrate at the festivities. When they go, everyone recognizes Sam as the soldier. Suzie, however, is the unrecognized soldier, fighting for her family on an emotional battlefield.

"You never know when you will have to look so far into your soul that you are not sure if you can go on," Suzie explained. "But if you keep walking through the smoke and are lucky enough to have a hand to hold, you'll start to see the light that is on the other side. And on that other side, miracles can happen."

She is thrilled by the progress they've made and optimistic about what the future holds for her family, but she knows she needs to continue to seek help.

"I participate in online support groups for spouses and caregivers of wounded warriors," she said, "and get support through my friends, family members, and my own therapist."

The Invictus Games have brought competition and camaraderie back to Sam's life. Instead of living inside of memories, he has a new life, with new challenges and new passions. No one is invincible, but in the battle of their lives, Sam and Suzie refuse to be defeated.

SHEILA: KEEPING FAITH

"You're not wounded."

Like many young combat veterans, Dan doesn't have obvious physical injuries, so he doesn't fit the description of what most people think a disabled combat veteran looks like. He's a strapping man with curly hair, horn-rimmed glasses, and an easy smile. One day he was wearing a Wounded Warriors T-shirt when someone confronted him and asked him why he was wearing the shirt.

"You're not wounded," the man said in an accusing tone.

Those words haunt Dan's wife Sheila to this day.

Would that person have been so quick to judge if he knew that Dan had been involved in multiple IED blasts during his deployments? Would that person have been so sure of his accusation if he were aware that Dan had been placed on 100 percent disability? Or if he'd been in the doctor's office when Dan was told that the reason he couldn't remember things or complete more than one task at a time was because he'd lost part of his brain function?

What if that man also knew that Dan had flown fifty-four Hero Flights, the air transports that bring dead soldiers, sailors, airmen, and Marines back to the United States in flagged caskets? Or if he knew Dan had experienced the strange hell of having to physically piece body parts back together so that the families of the fallen would have a complete body to bury? What if he'd known that when Dan had been forced into an early retirement with a medical discharge, he was depressed for months?

"You're not wounded."

Would that man have had the audacity to say that to his face if he'd sat at Dan's side during the migraine-filled days and insomnia-wracked nights? What if he walked in on Dan, as Sheila had done, while he was cradling a shotgun and preparing to end his life, convinced it was the only way to end his suffering? Would that have convinced the man that her husband was wounded?

Dan didn't "look wounded" to Sheila either when they met in his hometown of Kona, Hawaii, about twenty miles from where she was living. Dan was on leave from his duty station at Fort Hood in Texas, to assist his mother during her cancer treatments. Back then Sheila was a tall, dark beauty with a waterfall of hair. She was drawn immediately to Dan's obvious kindness. His trim physique didn't hurt, either.

On their second date, Dan confided that he had some "issues" due to the nature of his work as a medic in the Army.

"If you don't want to date me," he told her, "I'll understand."

But it was too late. Although Sheila knew being in a relationship with someone in the military could be hard—especially since they lived so far apart—she'd already fallen madly in love with Dan after their first date.

She'd never felt so relaxed around someone before. He was so easygoing and spontaneous, and she loved that he was attracted to her work ethic and admired her commitment to working full time while finishing her college degree. She was responsible and compassionate, wonderfully levelheaded and calm, and he loved that about her. He arranged impromptu dates, such as going to the beach to watch the sunset. They had a passionate love affair for the remaining two weeks that he was home on leave. There was no turning back.

A year later, they were married in a court wedding with no honeymoon. Then he deployed again. When he returned home from Afghanistan in February of 2012, his symptoms were worse than before, but Sheila didn't see it. She was so overjoyed to have him home again, in her arms, that she ignored the warning signs.

One of Dan's responsibilities was to prepare injured personnel to be medically evacuated. He gave them morphine to ease their pain and help keep them alive on their journeys. If they were already deceased, he prepared the bodies for travel, which could mean identifying body parts and gathering them together.

He routinely had to clean bodies, tag them around the neck or big toe, and load them into bags. Sometimes he had to forcefully stuff limbs already stiff with rigor mortis into body bags.

It's a little-known fact that medical personnel have some of the highest rates of PTS. In addition to trying to save the lives of America's soldiers, they are often put in positions where they are trying to save the lives of *enemy* combatants that have killed U.S. personnel. Other times, medics are called upon to fight and kill the enemy, when their instinct is to save them. These traumatic memories and conflicted feelings can stay with them for a lifetime.

One of the greatest challenges for veterans returning from Iraq and Afghanistan is to convey how these conflicts radically differ from images people have of war. The word itself—"war"—contributes to public misunderstanding of what young veterans have faced. The conflicts in Afghanistan, Iraq, and Syria are not wars between two countries. In fact, the military calls them "counterinsurgency operations." In such conflicts, the traditional boundaries between enemy combatants and civilians are almost completely blurred, and there are no front lines or safe havens. U.S. troops now fight against an enemy that could be anyone and anywhere. Even children or pregnant women potentially present lethal danger, since anyone could be hiding a bomb, a grenade, or the trigger to an IED. The lack of a clear enemy in the mission can intensify the moral confusion of war for soldiers: who is the "bad guy" and who is the "good guy"?

When Dan returned from his last six-month deployment, he was clearly traumatized. He begged not to be redeployed and was given a medical discharge. After he came home for good, Sheila jumped in to do whatever she could to kick-start his healing process. She helped her husband get the medication he needed: mood stabilizers, anxiety inhibitors, and Botox for his chronic migraines. She also made sure that he got counseling to help him transition to civilian life. But she found herself fighting everything from the convoluted systems of the VA to her husband's stony silence and powerful depression. It was an uphill battle.

Then the moment came when she wondered if she'd lost the battle for good. Sheila didn't know Dan during his first suicide attempt, but his second attempt happened in 2014—two years into their marriage, on the very day Sheila found out she was pregnant. While she was in the house, watching wide-eyed as the plus sign appeared on the pregnancy test, she heard a rattle in the garage and ran out to see what the noise was. She found Dan hanging from the rafters. She had to cut him down with rose clippers.

It was a terrifying wake-up call. She'd had no idea he was in such a dark place. Because she didn't know the signs to watch for, she hadn't been able to see Dan's wounds or read his suicidal thoughts.

Looking back on that moment, Sheila uses the analogy of infidelity. When your spouse cheats on you, you have to learn how to trust all over again. Even after you've done that, you still wonder, in the back of your mind, if it will happen again. After finding Dan in the garage, she worried constantly about her husband. How would she know if he hit rock bottom again? What could she do to keep him from sinking so low? Or was it all completely out of her control?

"At times," Sheila admitted, "I felt like the cards were stacked against us, that finding stability in all that despair was impossible."

But instead of giving up, she chose to take action. Dan's suicide attempt motivated Sheila to study the stresses that some returning combat warriors experienced so that she could try to understand what her husband was going through. And even when their relationship got rocky, she refused to give up. She admitted to consoling herself with food during the darkest times, and had put on weight due to stress eating. But otherwise, she focused on her strengths, embracing an attitude of "give just to give." She focused on serving the person she loved with the gift of selflessness, and by doing so she received as much as she gave.

"Back in England, my mom had abandoned my dad," she said, "so I knew I could never do the same. My dad taught me loyalty and when I give, I give 100 percent. My mom took my dad for granted, and I won't do that with my husband. I am so grateful to have him."

Although it's tempting to question the struggle, answers aren't going to accomplish the hard work of caring for her husband. "The truth is, we don't need answers. We need faith, and lots of it."

That faith and perseverance has rewarded Sheila with progress. Now Dan maintains a calendar for his appointments and meds, tries hard to be more communicative about his struggles, and has enrolled in school. The GI Bill is allowing him to seek a degree so that he can get back into the workforce as an X-ray technician.

"This is so important, because not working devastated his self-esteem," Sheila said. "School is just the first step for Dan, but it's a big one."

Sheila has a large family, all of whom moved to the U.S. from England when she was a small child, and she relies on them for support. She and Dan live with her grandfather, who is also a veteran and is hugely supportive. Being around him has had an amazing impact on Dan, who never knew his own father. They live next door to Sheila's dad and close to her four siblings, so there is always someone around to help out with Dan and Sheila's infant son.

"Having a son has been a ray of sunshine in our lives," she said.

Sheila believes their baby boy has given her husband a new lease on life. Now their home is filled with the joy that a baby brings—as well as new responsibilities. Dan watches their son while Sheila is at work three days a week. This gives father and son an opportunity to bond, and if Dan needs help there is always a friendly family member close by.

Last summer they took their belated honeymoon to Yosemite National Park. Experiencing the outdoors together, they were able to recapture the sense of adventure and spontaneity that marked the early days of their romance. The vacation invigorated them. It showed them both how far they have come and how much they have to look forward to.

Sheila anticipates the day when she can say to her husband, "You're not wounded—anymore."

LEXI: MIRACLE OF A DAUGHTER'S WISH

When Lexi first met Jared in 2006, everyone called him the life of the party. Boisterous, confident, and charming, he simply "radiated happiness." And happiness was exactly what Lexi needed at that moment. Fresh from a painful divorce, Lexi was down—down on herself and down on love. Yet she could not resist Jared's infectious laugh or his joyful approach to life, and she found that she wanted to be around him all of the time.

Once the two realized that the attraction was mutual, they became inseparable, marrying swiftly and having Teddy, an adorable baby boy. Two years later they had Chelsea. Then in the fall of 2010, with their daughter only two years old, Jared was deployed to Afghanistan. Lexi was nervous about the separation, but she took heart in the knowledge that Jared's job would rarely place him on the front lines. Jared was a logistics man for the Marines. He coordinated supplies, trucks, and transport—whatever needed to get organized, he was the man with the plan.

At first, Jared loved his assignment, and he was good at it. But it didn't take long for him to realize that part of being the logistics man was coordinating transportation for both the seriously injured and the soldiers who had died in battle. He was literally the man who would say a prayer over a fallen soldier's dead body and place the coffin on a plane back to America.

Soon the losses began to pile up. During the seven months of his deployment, Jared had to place twenty-five coffins on planes and coordinate care for more than one hundred severely injured men, most of whom were amputees. There was a time when he sent six coffins home in a single week. The stress of the job was already beginning to take a toll when he himself sustained an injury. He was driving near a local market when his vehicle hit an IED. Within seconds, his life and his world were turned upside down. Jared is not sure how long he was knocked unconscious, but he knows he woke up to people yelling his name, trying to get everyone out of the vehicle—and fast.

As he escaped the vehicle and righted himself, Jared assured the others that he felt fine. His shoulder ached a little, but it seemed like the kind of thing that would pass. This brush-off was typical of the way he coped while on deployment: stuff down any pain or discomfort and keep moving. And he continued in this way until he returned home to San Diego at the end of his tour.

He was delighted to reunite with Lexi, Teddy, and Chelsea in early 2011, and at first the family went through a glorious honeymoon phase. Daddy had returned, and he was in one piece. They needed time to bond and get to know one another all over again. Lexi was elated and everything seemed good.

However, she began to see that the man she had sent off to war had come back a very different person. Just as Lexi was catching on to some signs of his growing inner darkness, Jared was deployed on a peacekeeping mission to Jordan for a couple of months. When he returned from Jordan, a permanent cloud seemed to envelop him. He didn't want to go outside and stayed cooped up indoors for days at a time. He forgot things, and his temper would flare up in a flash.

Living on base and deeply immersed in the culture of the other Marines and their families, Lexi began to witness a disturbing trend. Many returning from combat were exhibiting signs of deep internal pain and were turning to drinking and drugs to calm their nerves.

"Lots of men didn't come back right," she told the group at SPA Day. "I saw most marriages crumble within that first six months."

Then Jared, who had once been a jovial social drinker, began to abuse alcohol in a serious way. Lexi would come home and find him drunk or passed out. She knew his dependence was growing, but when she brought it up, Jared would either drink less for just long enough to appease her or flat out deny that he had a problem. They functioned in this way for several months, until they hit a moment that changed Lexi's view of their entire relationship.

They were having fun at an outdoor concert in her hometown of Cleveland during the summer of 2012, but she eventually noticed that Jared had been drinking hard, and it was showing. He started to pick a fight as they left the venue. They argued as they walked. They were so involved in their fight that Lexi didn't look where she was walking, and she fell into a large hole left behind by the crew that had set up the stages. She was covered in mud, banged up, and scared when she called up to Jared, asking for help to get out. But severely intoxicated and fueled up on anger, he yelled at her, "Just deal with it," and walked off, leaving her there. Her knee had been dislocated, and she was in a lot of pain. As she watched him storm off, she thought, *He just wants to burn the whole world down.*

With the help of some other concertgoers, Lexi got herself out of the hole, but couldn't find Jared. She called for him, walking around the grounds shouting his name. Then she took to her cell phone and called everyone she knew—but no Jared. Finally, she headed home and called the police, who notified the highway patrol. They found him at a bar a few hours later, totally incoherent, and brought him home.

The next day, Lexi tried to talk to Jared about the incident, but he didn't remember any of it. That was the breaking point for Lexi. He had left her in a hole—literally and figuratively—one too many times. She wanted nothing more than an intact family, but she could no longer live this way.

Seeing how much pain he had caused Lexi, Jared acknowledged that he had to give up drinking—and he never drank from that day forward. The lack of alcohol did help their healing a bit. But the issues that had led to the drinking were still there, lurking under the surface, nagging at Jared's mind, driving him crazy. He couldn't sleep. He felt tremendous guilt.

Why had he been able to return home and have a good life with his wife and kids? Why had so many of his friends had their legs or arms blown off? Why hadn't he been one of the men who got escorted back in a coffin? Jared was plagued by the belief that he could have and should have done more. He shouldn't have been doing his job as the logistics man; he should've been out there on the front lines, saving his buddies from harm.

Seeing her husband sink further into depression, without the escape that alcohol had given him, Lexi begged Jared to get some help. She went to his battalion commander and told him she was truly worried, but was told that Jared had to *want* help for them to help him.

Shortly after that frustrating meeting with the battalion commander, Lexi and Jared had a truly wonderful day together. But then Jared's mood shifted suddenly, just as Lexi was beginning to feel a sliver of hope for their future.

It had been one of the lighter days for Lexi, her husband Jared, and their three-year-old daughter Chelsea. A day when the sun shone through, and their lives seemed almost normal—lots of laughter, giggling, tickling, and joking around. Then, for some reason, a dark cloud began to creep into Jared's mind. Lexi had witnessed Jared's internal shift before, going from jovial and lighthearted to suspicious and aggressive.

That day, within minutes of the laughter fest, he tried to pick a fight. But the day had been too good, so Lexi wasn't having any of it. She wanted to relish the feeling that they were making progress on their marriage, so she scooped up her daughter and took her to Walmart. She wanted to stay away from the house for a few hours to let the cloud pass naturally.

When they were done shopping, Lexi offered, "Let's go get ice cream."

"No, Mommy, I want to go home now," Chelsea said.

Lexi acquiesced to her daughter. That decision would prove miraculous. She did not understand the full significance of her husband's shift until she and Chelsea returned home from Walmart. Then Lexi knew right away that something was not right. Jared was erratic. It looked as if he had tried to change clothes several times, and they had only been gone for an hour or so.

It wasn't until Lexi walked into the kitchen that it all made sense. He had recently filled a prescription for the antidepressant drug Cymbalta—and every single one of the new pills was gone.

She ran back to Jared, who was almost passed out on the couch.

"I'm calling nine-one-one," she said.

"No, don't call. Don't call. Please."

Jared was firm. He would not allow her to call for help. Lexi finally acquiesced, but she pulled her husband into the bathroom, where she made him throw up. She stayed up all night with him, helping him empty his stomach of the pills and walking with him to make sure he didn't fall into a sleep from which he might not wake up.

The next morning, he could no longer deny that there was something truly wrong, something that quitting drinking could not fix, and that it had to be dealt with right away. Both the Army and the Marines maintain wounded warrior programs to deal with special needs of wounded combat troops who still want to serve. Jared agreed to let Lexi reach out to these programs.

In 2013, Jared was admitted into the Wounded Warrior Battalion, and it changed their lives forever. In a setting designed for mutual support, Marines live together in barracks while receiving care and treatment. Those who recover sufficiently can return to full duty with their parent units. Others receive help with the transition to civilian life and VA care, and their families are supported through the process. Jared chose to move into civilian life.

Jared's health issues were finally taken seriously by professionals equipped to help him. He was admitted to a three-month, intensive inpatient center. Lexi, too, received therapy, which helped to address some of her own anger. After all they'd been through together, she found that she was furious at her husband for attempting to take his own life.

"He would have only caused us all that much more pain forever," she said.

She was outraged, yet she also knew that he was sick. She knew that he had to get his illness addressed, the way someone with cancer needed treatment. And finally she was able to see that she, too, deserved some care.

To this day, Lexi maintains the role of "the one that holds it all together." She has never really let herself fall apart. She has a stellar career in finance and manages a team of twenty-five. She balances motherhood, career, self-care, and the care of her husband. She keeps it all together because it's in her nature to do so, but also because she has to.

But it's not all stress and strain. Lexi finds relief knowing just how far they have come toward healing. With both of them in therapy, she and Jared now have an easier time talking to one another about the most difficult issues.

She keeps herself grounded in gratitude, especially to her young daughter. Had she stayed out with Chelsea that day, Lexi feels certain that her husband would have succeeded in his suicide attempt.

"He could be gone. We almost lost him."

Lexi's greatest wish is that the worst is behind them and that more joy will rise to the surface for the man she fell in love with. Thanks to hard work, consistent support, and the premonition of a loving daughter, she patiently watches as her family's joy grows strong and true, slowly but surely.

* * *

In his book *Man's Search for Meaning*, Viktor Frankl illustrates the importance of finding purpose and direction in life. As an inmate in a Nazi concentration camp, he provided mental health care for his fellow prisoners, helping them deal with the shock and grief of their internment. He writes passionately and poetically about ways that each individual can search for and find meaning in life. He believes that "saying yes to life no matter what" inspires people to live and help others to have meaningful lives.

"What is to give light must endure burning," Frankl writes. Even in the most painful and dehumanizing of situations, he saw hope, just as Suzie, Sheila, and Lexi did. Even as their husbands grappled with hopelessness, they were able to tap into their inner strength to lift their loved ones out of the darkness.

CHAPTER 5

SEXUALITY: BATTLEFIELDS TO BEDROOMS

Sex is the seed, love is the flower, compassion is the fragrance.

—OSHO

"HOW OFTEN SHOULD we be having sex?"

That's the number one question the sex therapist received from the women who came to our most recent SPA Day support group. It sounds like a simple question, but it's actually quite complex. There was no way she could tell these women how often they "should" have sex—that depends on age, health, and a host of other things. But she did tell them about some eye-opening research on how often people are actually having sex in this country.

It turns out that for married couples under fifty years of age, the frequency (on average) is about twice a week. So now we know how often our neighbors may be having sex! Remember, though, these are just averages. Some couples are happy with more frequent sex, some with less. And that's really the point: it's not how much sex we are having that's important, but whether we and our partners are happy with the sex we're having.

After a relaxing massage, wine, and lunch, the women talked about their sex lives while the sex therapist facilitated the conversation. Because she was entertaining, warm, and kind, we all felt comfortable talking about this often taboo topic.

One woman compared sex to the frosting on a cake, calling it "the added bonus to a relationship." However, she added, "Sure, the other components, like friendship, compatibility, and similar values are the real glue that hold a relationship together, but I want to overcome the trauma and get back that intimacy, not just survive."

Continuing the food metaphor, another wife compared sex to pizza, saying, "Everyone has different tastes as to how much they want, what toppings, and whether they want to eat alone with their partner or in a group." The women all believed they were much more open-minded about sex than their parents had been. They accepted a range of diverse sexual activities as being in the "normal and healthy" category.

Listening to wives and the counselor, I came to understand that lack of sex drive isn't unusual among PTS sufferers. More often than not, decreased libido is a side effect of the medications given to combat PTS symptoms. Some PTS medications regulate the level of the chemical serotonin in the brain, and serotonin plays an important role in sexual functioning. While taking these medications, many people report delayed or absent orgasms and reduced interest in sex. Since their husbands may only want to make love a couple of times per month or less, some women advise "seizing the moment" when the PTS sufferer is open to sex. Husbands suffering from PTS can shift from one mood to another without notice, so the window for intimacy might be quite small.

But it isn't always medications that kill the mood. In addition to lack of serotonin and unexpected mood swings, partners are often nervous about sex after a severe injury. Anxious people produce excessive amounts of certain hormones that negatively affect sexual functioning by constricting blood vessels and blood flow, both of which are important to sexual health. Many wives have told me it wasn't uncommon for their men to have difficulty achieving or maintaining an erection, a problem that can arise from not only emotional problems, but also circulatory issues.

When someone we love is wounded, we feel hurt, too. Many wives are hit by what I call "PTS shrapnel." After long deployments, both partners want to feel the other person's loving touch, but when the husband is injured, what's wanted and what's possible might not align. They all tend to agree that good sex starts with good love, but they also accept that they might not be able to rekindle intimacy right away.

As the conversation continued, the wives talked about the solutions and workarounds they were using to get through sexual dry spells. Here are six options the ladies discussed:

1. Lead a celibate life.

Suzie said, "It wasn't that important to me to begin with. I channel my love on a more spiritual level. I love him not for who he is physically, but for his soul. I enjoy his affection without the sex." This was a controversial opinion that some other wives pushed back against, but a few agreed. "I can't just accept total celibacy," Julie said, "but I'm fine with having sex less often. Even going months without, if that's what it takes to make both of us feel comfortable."

2. Pleasure yourself.

Julie told us, "I can please myself. Self-pleasure is good for us! And I'm not stepping outside the bonds of my marriage, having an affair. There are so many toys and porn movies available it's no longer a challenge to please myself or experiment with adult play. It takes the pressure off everyone." Fiona agreed, saying, "An apple a day keeps the doctor away, and I've learned an orgasm a day keeps the stress away."

3. Step outside the marriage.

The women actually talked about this openly, though there were plenty of flushed cheeks and downcast eyes. Carla opened the topic, saying, "I treated myself to a solo day at the spa and got a massage with benefits. Men have been getting 'happy ending' massages for years, so I thought I'd give it a try." She told us that she did her best to be subtle, since she didn't want to get kicked out of the spa or get her masseuse in trouble. She parted her legs a bit and gave little moans of approval when he moved his hand closer. It was thrilling because it was forbidden, like a scene out of *Sex and the City*. But she wasn't totally free of guilt. Was she being unfaithful in this act? "I feel like it's not really cheating because I didn't touch the masseuse or even look at him," she concluded. "He just pleased me with his hands as he was massaging my thighs."

Some women tossed around the idea of stepping outside their marriages with a boyfriend. Jane proposed to her husband the idea of having a boyfriend, and although the conversation was hard, it opened up some important channels of communication. "Kyle didn't like the idea *at all*, but talking about it made him see how our total lack of sex was affecting me," she said. Another woman had the opposite experience, and told the group, "My husband gave me permission to seek another lover." Since his injuries had made nearly all sexual activity difficult or impossible, he put this offer on the table in an effort to keep her happy and make sure she felt valued within the marriage. "I'm still thinking it over," she told us. "He said it might eventually be something we could talk about and share intimately—he might like to hear about how I'm seeking pleasure with another man. And I'm tempted. But it's a big leap of faith to take, you know?"

Another woman said she'd read my book *Unbridled*—a memoir about my journey to self-discovery after my marriage fell apart—and asked if she could go to lunch with me. Having read that I had cheated on my husband, she felt comfortable sharing her story. Over lunch, she admitted that she had been having a secret affair with a coworker. She was wracked with guilt about it, but had felt so alone, and this man had been there to console her. Eventually, consolation turned to attraction. She felt she was now in love with this new man, but also felt trapped since her husband was confined to a wheelchair and they had two young children together. She told me she wanted to talk with me because she knew I'd understand.

Although we did have an experience in common, it made me sad to hear her story. Earlier in my life, if I'd had access to some of the information these ladies shared, I might not have made the mistakes I did, including my affair. If I had addressed the problems in my marriage with friends and a therapist—like these brave wives were doing—I might have dealt with things more honestly. I opted to run away and take a lover when things weren't going well at home, and it not only damaged me, the secret keeper, but also hurt my husband and children.

My situation was much different than this young woman's. My husband was self-sufficient, both physically and financially, and my children were teenagers, not toddlers. The guilt this woman felt for leaving a young, disabled husband who couldn't take care of himself made her situation so much more difficult. Opening up to me gave her someone to talk to and an opportunity to begin sharing what it was like to feel guilty. Telling our stories helps us begin to heal and discover that we are not alone.

4. Leave the marriage.

Lisa started to cry as she said, "I'm twenty-five and can't live a celibate life and can't live a secretive life. My husband would *never* be okay with porn, a massage with benefits, or a lover." She told me after her SPA Day massage that it had been the first time anyone had touched her sensuously in years. She did not want to give up sexual intimacy for the rest of her life. I tried to reassure her that passion can ebb and flow within a long-term marriage. But I hated to think that she'd never have sex with her husband again, especially since it was clearly important to her.

Mary said, "I know that PTS often shows up as depression and lack of sex drive, but my husband outwardly expresses his rage through abuse. I feel used, even raped. The sex is all about him. There is no intimacy and connection. It's a form of masturbating at my expense when he uses sex to let off steam. I don't want to have sex with him or even be married to him." Mary told us her husband "had reckless sex with lots of women" and that he told her these other women didn't mean anything; having sex with them was just his way of getting high and escaping. "I've got a son in grade school who sees this man as a role model," Mary went on. "This man who drinks and rages and sleeps around. I'm just not sure it's worth it to stay with him."

5. Renew the contract.

Lexi added, "I renegotiated how often we had sex when he came home and we recommitted ourselves to our relationship. Figuring out the frequency helped us understand each other's needs, desires, emotional wounds, and barriers. Understanding when being sexual felt good for both of us brought us a deeper understanding and led to a desire to hear and please each other."

Shannon explained that she, too, wanted to "know" her partner. The Bible says to know someone is to be intimate (have sex) with him or her. It's hard to be intimate with a man who won't share himself. Shannon watched her husband go from nonverbal and nearly paralyzed to an active, successful businessman. But even though they were having sex, she felt like true intimacy was a missing piece in their relationship.

These women want to understand their men, hear about what happened when they were away, and bring out the best in them. They believe that sex will help them to bring out the best in each other. The best thing that wives of wounded warriors—and, really, all women—can do is to get to know their partners—what turns them on, what turns them off—in all areas of life.

6. Take yourself off the market.

Sheila looked down, her dark hair obscuring her face. "I've gained 100 pounds since all this happened. Food is my comfort, my pleasure, my sex. I've made myself so fat my husband wouldn't be interested in me, and I'm relieved," she admitted.

"The Prozac kills my sex drive and gaining all this weight, I don't have to worry about anyone wanting to have sex with me, including my husband. I've dealt with him coming home wounded and with his drug use, so I don't even have the energy to think about sex."

Food can be a form of self-medication—it's comforting and a more socially acceptable form of addiction than drugs. Sheila knew that she was channeling her stress in a way that directly impacted her physical health. She knew, but she couldn't seem to stop.

* * *

For these women, telling their stories isn't just venting. Acknowledging their own feelings helps them to move forward, to deal with their lives in ways that are constructive and not destructive. I truly believe that what we don't bring forth will destroy us. If we don't own our feelings, we'll act on them, hide them, or bury them, all of which can lead to depression and worse. When we have the ability to accept the reality we live in, we can adapt in healthier ways.

As difficult as it is at first, we need to learn to be truthful in our sexual relationships, partnerships, and marriages, to talk about what's not working and find ways to make improvements together. We must adapt as a team and keep the lines of communication as open as possible. Because all the tricks in the world—date nights, sex toys, and porn movies—won't work if both partners aren't willing to know each other. Once the wife can talk about what's she's going through, she can find healthy ways to cope. Once the husband knows what his wife is feeling, he can adapt and respond. Think of the metaphor of dancing: two people in sync, harmonizing and communicating. This is what leads to great sex—using your bodies to talk to and understand each other.

Communing is the best aspect of a relationship, and sex is part of that communing. The art of loving—finding a path back to genuine love—can lead to great sex, even for couples living with relationships that involve altered bodies and minds.

Read on to hear from Kelly, whose sex life with her injured partner has become a very pleasant surprise, and Kendal, who learned to help her husband channel his sexual energy in a new and thrilling way after he returned home from war with emotional scars.

KELLY: KISSING AND TELLING

As the result of an IED blast, Kelly's husband Seth had not only lost both his legs, but also been castrated. Any man who has ever been kicked in the balls on a playing field or in a fight will cringe at the thought of such an unimaginable blow.

In the current conflicts in Afghanistan and the Middle East, the enemy tends to plant its IEDs on fences, roadsides, or anywhere else, positioning them so that the blast often hits the legs and genitals of passing soldiers. Multiple-limb amputation with genitourinary (GU) wounds are common injuries in this war. Blown-away balls has become the new "signature wound."

I was inspired to do my own research into this "signature wound" of America's latest wars. I read journalistic accounts, online anecdotes, and narratives in medical journals. The rumors I heard about infantrymen making do-not-resuscitate pacts with medics—asking their combat buddies not to save them if their sex organs were a casualty—really got to me. They thought they would rather be dead than castrated.

Seth suffered his injury while on a foot patrol in Afghanistan in 2013 and returned home within days to get medical attention on U.S. soil. A Native American woman with a no-nonsense disposition, Kelly never imagined that her warrior, just out of high school, would take an unlucky step that would castrate him. But what happened afterward surprised her even more.

"The best sex I've ever had is with a man who most people think can't have it," Kelly said, flaunting her curvy body with a twinkle in her eye. "That's an extremely personal thing to blurt out at SPA Day—and something I've only shared with my sister and best girlfriends."

Phantom pain is common in amputees, but Kelly says she can still feel her husband's missing limbs, too. Because some parts physically don't work as well as others, she feels his love through the sparkle in his eyes, the touch of his hand, and the way his whole body wants to be next to hers.

"They say sex takes place in the mind, and I can feel every part of his body excited to be with me, not just his dick or his missing legs," she explained.

When Kelly's husband was recovering from his injuries, he pretty much wrote off ever having a satisfying sexual relationship again. But their sexual experiences in the aftermath were a revelation, and brought out Kelly's sassy side. Today she'll brag that she's having the kind of sex most women would envy.

And it turns out she is not an anomaly—other wives have said the same thing.

"My husband lost some leverage in the act of lovemaking, but gained some serious flair in the number of positions he can now maneuver his body into, especially if he removes his prosthetics," Carla said.

Another woman, Kendal, spoke of the necessity of finding humor in their circumstances, but it can be hard to stay lighthearted when facing the difficulties of the recovery process. All the wives I've spoken to admit that going from the battlefield into the bedroom with GU wounds (burned, shot, mangled, and in some cases amputated sex organs) is, at the beginning, anguishing for both their partners and them. Even though the doctors tell the couple that it is okay to take it slowly, even though wives try hard to reignite passion, the transition can be a trying, harrowing experience, and the lack of sexual intimacy can threaten the health of their marriages.

After commiserating about overlapping experiences, Kelly picked up her story again. "My husband felt disfigured and ugly, and assumed I must see him as unattractive as well," she told the other women. "At first, sexual contact felt more painful than good for him, so he pushed me away when I tried to start something. But luckily for our marriage, I refused to take no for an answer."

Because both the severity and the frequency of GU wounds among recent vets are unprecedented, there is no road map yet to guide injured vets and their partners back to intimacy. No manual exists on the do's and don'ts of having sex with this type of disability. Until the VA and military medicine catch up, these newly injured veterans have to rely on their imaginations and resourcefulness.

"I refused to accept the 'I don't know' answer the VA doctor gave when I asked, 'When will my husband want to have sex again?'" Kelly said. "With my marriage in jeopardy and the possibility of having a child at risk, I took his sexual recovery into my own hands. And take my word for it, I was surprised by the imaginative and resourceful ways we found to overcome the challenges of a GU injury."

Those challenges are many and varied. They can include inability to maintain an erection or ejaculate, as well as a lack of sensation in the lower body—which brings a whole separate subset of problems. If the husband can't feel what he's doing, he's also unable to feel how hard or at what angle he's pressing against his partner. Many of the women told me they need to ride their husbands so they can control the intensity.

Some couples worked together with fertility clinics to save and freeze the husband's sperm ahead of time so that they could still have biological children together even if he sustained a GU injury. But this is a very expensive procedure and not something every couple considers before deployment.

When Seth returned home with his GU injury, Kelly set to work finding a private urologist who specialized in penile implants. She connected with a doctor who had performed many sex-change operations on civilians, and he reconstructed a new penis and testicles for Seth. After the surgery and with the help of testosterone supplements, Seth was able to ejaculate, but he was unable to produce new sperm. Kelly was so grateful that she had convinced him to save sperm before his deployment.

If you tell an 18-year-old that he'll get a chance to play with guns, receive a college education, and be a hero, he might be convinced to sign up with the military. But rarely does the recruitment office mention the dangers of GU wounds, a class of injury that often leaves warriors unable to have children or have typical, easy sex lives when they return. Kevlar vests protect warriors' chests, and helmets shield their heads, but their limbs, groins, and genitals are almost always exposed and unprotected. Men who return home with GU wounds face many obstacles in the bedroom, and even when couples are able to overcome those obstacles together, doubt can creep back in. Wives find themselves wondering:

"Will I be attractive to him again?"

"Will I be able to sexually satisfy my partner?"

"Forget about my partner; will *I* ever feel sexual pleasure again?"

"Those are questions I can answer with some authority," Kelly said. "Because I know from my own experience, and now from hearing similar stories from other couples, that great sex is *not* out of reach just because the sex organs no longer work the same. In fact, my husband and I have learned that when it comes to having what we call 'transcendent sex,' the condition of the physical body is almost immaterial. And not only is good sex still possible, the best sex of your life can be still to come. I share my story as evidence that anyone—ready, willing, able, or disabled—can experience ecstatic, knock-your-socks-off sex. All you need is a loving partner and a little knowledge."

She advised the women to find aphrodisiacs that work for both partners—anything from thrilling activities like riding roller coasters for a shared endorphin rush to watching sensual movies together can excite. She also reminded everyone that for men, the pleasure can be in the erection, not the orgasm, since once they climax it's all over. This means that the majority of the pleasure they experience is in the potential, the arousal. And since sex is often better for many women when men don't rush the orgasm but prolong the high, this is great news.

Men don't always need genital stimulation to become aroused; smelling, kissing, or caressing attracts them to their lover. Kelly explained that it's very easy to make her husband's penis hard, and if the woman is on top and in control, what you lack in one area you can make up in another. Although some men with GU wounds can't actually feel their penises, seeing their wives getting off can bring them to climax from the connection.

Kelly continued, "We rebuilt our intimacy by role-playing, watching erotic movies, and buying the latest adult toys. We keep up with cutting-edge treatments from Western medicine as well as taking advantage of ancient healing modalities from the East, like acupuncture and pranic healing."

She explained that they bring into the bedroom the latest of what present-day pharmacology has to offer to overcome the limitations of an amputee's physical anatomy. But perhaps more importantly, they apply and experiment with sexual fantasies and secret fetishes. Sharing sexual intimacy is what creates closeness for them as a couple. "Sprinkle in love, and it adds up to some mind-blowing sex with a man who once believed his combat injury had blown his chances for ever getting it the way he does now."

Kelly and her husband are a few years down the road now and agree their sex life is better than it ever was. And beyond the satisfying physical relationship, fighting a battle they weren't sure they'd win means they've forged an emotional bond that is rock solid. After seeing her warrior overcome the battle of a disability and come out stronger than ever mentally and physically, she's more attracted to him than ever.

"There is nothing that can break us now," she assured us, flashing a bright smile.

Keeping the details of one's sex life private is, I believe, generally a good policy. But knowing that American servicemen are coming home with genital wounds that affect their chances for having fulfilling intimate relationships, I've shifted my thinking. I've come to feel an almost patriotic duty to unbolt the bedroom door and help wives of wounded warriors, like Kelly, open up about their relationships with injured war veterans.

Kelly's story is a message of hope for servicemen suffering these catastrophic wounds in the prime of life, and for the spouses they're coming home to. Her story tells them to rest assured: great—even phenomenal—sex does not have to be a casualty of war.

KENDAL: TAKING THE REINS

On September 11, 2001, Kendal's brother-in-law was in the South Tower of the World Trade Center. Kendal watched her television in horror as the towers erupted into a blazing fire and crumbled to the ground.

"I felt scared and isolated sitting all alone at home, with my husband at work as an EMT." Terror had struck home in the most personal way possible, and Kendal was anguished and enraged. The events of 9/11 and the death of her brother-in-law were among the reasons she supported Larry, her husband of two years, when he said he wanted to enlist in the Army.

Larry's fierce response to his brother's death highlighted how war can transform love into brutal action. She knew he wanted revenge. He volunteered to go to Iraq, he said, not just to uphold American ideals, but to avenge his beloved brother who had been killed by Al Qaida terrorists. Larry threw himself into his military career, and in April 2003, he was sent on a dangerous mission to look for insurgents. While breaking down the door of a potential enemy home, he was shot at point-blank range. Though he was badly injured, his training kicked in and, even though he was bleeding profusely, he carried one of his injured comrades to safety. He will never forget the images of that day—burning buildings, terrified faces, and his fellow soldiers broken and bleeding.

During the eight months her husband had been away on this deployment, Kendal had looked at her favorite wedding picture every single day. Taken at a romantic winery in Southern California, it showed the two of them holding hands, her long, brown hair flowing down her back, her figure petite next to his strong, protective frame. Kendal saw her husband as a fierce, mischievous, blue-eyed bear, a handsome man she likened to a strapping warrior. Living boldly in the world was just what came naturally to him.

"Our friends watched the Iraq debacle on TV like they were watching the weather report," she recalled. "For them, it was just a momentary distraction that stubbornly refused to go away. For me, it was a senseless and horrifying spectacle that couldn't end soon enough."

That April, Larry came home with his body and mind in pieces. His arm had to be amputated just above the elbow after two surgeries failed to save it. He lost his left eye and suffered multiple face and chest wounds.

And those were just the wounds that could be seen. Clearly, underneath all the bandages, Larry was not the same person. The man who returned to Kendal's bed was anxious, jumpy, mistrustful, and moody. Everything in their lives was off kilter. Sleeping meant night terrors. Horrific images of war would cause Larry to bolt upright, his eyes wide with fear. In an altered state, he'd immediately search the bedroom for an M16 that was never there.

"Larry and I are both survivors," she said. "I expected him to put the war behind him. It's part of our culture to believe that people can kill the enemy on the battlefield without physical and psychological vulnerability. Larry watched his friends get blown to bits. He was expected to shed a couple of manly tears and get on with his life. The fact is, Larry came home nothing like the man he was before he left."

Soon she found that his lovemaking appetites had shifted, too. If he wanted sex, it was aggressive and uncaring, just a release of tension. War had transformed his relationship with love and passion. He wanted to combine sex and violence, and the two together were his biggest turn-on. He'd ask her to resist as he ripped her clothes off. He was overpowering, and at times she found she liked it. He wanted her so badly it turned her on. But other times, the desperation of Larry's advances made her feel sullied and dirty. Kendal felt there was no consideration for her feelings, no loving touch. It was as if he were just using her body.

He even ordered her to "bird dog" for him, demanding she have a threesome with him as if she were under his chain of command. When that didn't work, he seduced her into it—he got her to let him watch her with another girl, and then he joined in.

He was insatiable in bed. He insisted on having sex at least two times a day.

He'd returned from combat with a hunger, a desire to restore his inner life that only the intensity of erotic arousal could fulfill. Although some of it was thrilling, eventually Kendal could no longer tolerate being his receptacle. When she tried to talk to him about what was going on, he could only say that he'd been so deeply steeped in death for eight months that he needed sex to feel in touch with life again.

She sought out counseling, and in 2004 began exploring her feelings in a safe space with a therapist. Over time, she learned that she did like his aggressiveness sometimes and occasionally enjoyed being controlled. It reminded her of *Fifty Shades of Grey*, the titillating push-and-pull of a dominant-submissive relationship. But she didn't want this all the time. Unfortunately, Larry did.

Her therapist explained that you can take the men out of war, but it's harder to take the war out of men. After they come home, they often try to connect with their softer sides by making love, but sometimes it can't be found there. The lust for bloodletting awakened by war often transfers to their sexuality back at home, since both involve strong emotional and physical responses. The survivors often do not feel shame, even if their partners feel debased—they feel justified, or as if they are acting out of necessity. As Larry had tried to express to her, they begin to see sex as a way to counterbalance all the death they have seen.

At first, Larry was unaware of Kendal's discomfort, or maybe, Kendal thought, he just didn't care. But eventually, he saw that his new appetites were driving them apart. He said that while overseas, he had become strangely addicted to the violence of war, and at home he sought his fix in sex.

"I had a terrible love of war," he said. "So I tried to combine love and war in our bedroom." Larry admitted that he had witnessed servicemen rape civilians during his deployment. Some of his fellow soldiers told him they saw rape as a way to exact revenge against the whole culture. He claimed he never raped anyone in Iraq, but after experiencing his new obsession with aggressive sex, Kendal wondered if he was sharing the full story with her.

Then one cold night in 2005, Larry opened up.

"I shot a man to death up close, and it gave me a hard-on," he told her. "The experience was far more intimate and erotic than love or sex can ever be." Larry said he found pleasure in combat, a release of primal aggression parallel to the orgasmic discharge. He explained that, after this experience, it helped him get aroused to think of her as a dirty, naughty bad girl, even a whore. With all the death and war he had seen, he no longer wanted vanilla sex; he wanted to feel the gritty lust of something slightly wrong, temptingly forbidden. Being a warrior, he wanted to conquer, and physical touch without aggressive sex became intolerable, even impossible.

At times, sex was the only connection they had, so Kendal tried to enjoy the intensity. Her work in therapy had taught her that it was okay to give in to this role-playing game when she wanted to. She hoped lust led to love. At the same time, she knew in her heart that Larry didn't feel truly close to her—in or out of bed.

In fact, Larry had used the mantra "Don't get too close to anyone" to get through the endless cycle of losing friends throughout his deployment. Back home, he had not switched off that survival mechanism, and it began to drive a wedge between him and Kendal. He wasn't able to experience love because he'd closed himself off from the possibility of emotional pain. It was as if Larry's ability to trust anyone or anything had vanished altogether. On a daily basis, Kendal said, "Larry was reclusive, withdrawn, emotionless—combative."

Then there was the isolating behavior. In Larry's mind, family and friends always seemed to want, want, and want more. They wanted the couple to spend time with them, they wanted everything to go back to normal, they wanted the couple to be happy and feel okay about the war. They meant well, but they didn't understand. Consequently, Larry pulled away more and more into icy solitude, trusting no one, seeing no one. At the age of thirty-one, Kendal didn't know if she could spend the rest of her life in this cold, lonely vacuum of a marriage.

But things took a turn in March 2006, when the two went out for a drive with Larry at the wheel. He was generally okay to drive, but sometimes when he saw roadkill, his mind interpreted it as a body bag, and he would begin hyperventilating. On that quiet spring day, he pulled the car over, but not because of anything he saw. Something, suddenly, had cracked within him. He broke down and sobbed.

Kendal held Larry as the worst of his flashbacks came pouring out of him. He told her that on one occasion, when the soldiers were clearing houses for insurgents, they took all the jewelry, TVs, or money they could find and brought them back to the barracks. Once, he stood guard outside of a house while two of his "friends" raped the women and young girls inside. Larry didn't participate, or even watch, but he could hear the horrible grunts and screams from inside. Those sounds still haunted him.

It was time to get some help—and fast. The next day, Kendal called the VA hospital and made an appointment for counseling. At the end of a four-hour evaluation, the doctor told her that Larry was exhibiting symptoms of PTS, and with that diagnosis in hand, she was finally able to convince Larry to go to therapy on a regular basis.

"Larry knows that he is capable of hurting me physically, mentally, and emotionally," Kendal said. "Because of these awful flashbacks, he's afraid he might hit me in his sleep during a nightmare. He says he doesn't want to scare me with dark stories from Iraq, so he's kept it all inside. He doesn't trust authority or the system, and he's lost faith in goodness, justice, and fair play, so he's put up all these walls. But somewhere in there, he knows he can't just shut out the world and go completely numb, because I need him, and his family needs him."

Kendal was relieved that Larry would finally be dealing with his demons, and hoped it might help him be less tense and more open.

"In the beginning, the medications helped to control his anxiety and depression, so he could sit down and participate in talk therapy. But then he lost his sex drive completely," Kendal said.

She still held out hope that therapy would be the catalyst for real change. But life inched along, and nothing really seemed to get better at home. In fact, after almost two years of outpatient therapy, Larry continued to shake whenever an otherwise benign sight or sound triggered his PTS. Their sex life had gone from overwhelming to nonexistent. For Kendal and Larry, life had become intolerable and hopeless.

Then something miraculous and unexpected happened. And it was entirely by accident.

In the fall of 2006, on one of their weekly five-mile runs, Larry and Kendal encountered two women on horseback coming down the road toward them. A slow smile spread across Kendal's face. She had grown up riding horses, and when she was younger and life got tough, she had always found serenity in the pasture. Watching the two women, she was immediately transported back to her childhood barn, a local stable where she spent all of her free time. She could almost smell the rawhide, hay, sage, and sawdust, and feel the sense of freedom she used to have when she was riding. She and Larry stopped running, slowly approached one of the riders, and asked if they could touch her horse. After she nodded yes, they both, ever so gently, put their hands on the horse's neck. Soon they struck up a lively conversation with the women riders, who invited them back to their stable to see their other horses. The couple happily obliged.

As they followed the women to the barn, a warm comforting feeling rose within Kendal's chest. The snorts, the gentle swish of tails, and the clank of irons as stable hands flung saddles over the horses' backs brought all her wonderful memories rushing back. Larry knew nothing about horses, but had always been curious about them. Months later, he would say in couples therapy that being close to the animals, smelling them, hearing them breathe, and feeling their soft yet powerful necks brought him a feeling of connectedness he could barely explain. He said it was the first time since his deployment that he remembered feeling comfortable in his own skin.

Hearing this made perfect sense to Kendal. She had always felt that horses had a natural ability to accept anyone without judgment—and that included soldiers who might have seen or done horrifying things and come home with unsettling tastes. She believed that a horse's ability to express compassion and offer benevolent acknowledgment is an extraordinary gift to the humans who know and love them.

After that day at the barn, the couple came home hopeful. It took them less than a week to join a therapeutic riding center, where they began a friendship with a horse named Sundance.

"We felt safe with her. I know this sounds weird, but when I looked in her eyes, I felt like she knew who I was," Kendal said. "Our horse didn't know us from before the war. She didn't want anything from us, didn't expect anything. We didn't have to talk about our feelings; we could just feel them, and she was okay with it. She opened us up. When we realized she had started to trust us, we also realized that it was the first time since Larry had come home from the war that we truly felt like us, like we had gotten our old selves back."

Larry admitted that for him, some of the appeal was still rooted in thrill seeking. Horseback riding can be risky, and clinging to the back of a horse as it rockets through a field brings quite an adrenaline rush. Both he and Kendal were relieved and excited to have found a nonsexual way to feed their hunger for adventure, and to release some of the tension that life with PTS often brings.

Eight years after their first ride, Larry still finds extraordinary peace in the saddle. He enjoys sharing this experience with other veterans, and finds that although he doesn't always trust his doctors, he always trusts his vet comrades and the horses. After bonding with other soldiers in the war, he found the stables to be the perfect postservice setting in which to connect with those who shared his battlefield experiences. And for Kendal, the wide-open countryside life is full of possibilities, a place where her worries dissipate.

"The feeling," she said, "is beyond happiness."

As they both became stronger, Kendal discovered she wanted to devote her life to helping others. When Larry joined the police force as a motorcycle patrolman in 2014—another great way for him to express his love for protection and adventure—Kendal decided to get her certification in horse therapy. Far from the chaos of a war zone or the bedlam of the local VA medical center, Kendal helps in a nontraditional therapy program.

"The main focus of the program is helping veterans who have been diagnosed with PTS and TBI to interact in a safe and healing environment," she explained to me one afternoon when I visited her and Larry at the ranch where the program was held.

Most social settings for returning vets are overwhelming, Kendal noted. "Veterans tend to withdraw socially and isolate, which can lead to concerns of suicide."

The program provides a huge break from overwhelming input, and each veteran works individually with a horse and a therapist. In just six weeks, they progress from learning how to groom and saddle a horse, to cantering, to trail rides. From a mental health perspective, the program has been successful in breaking through the toughest of PTS symptoms, including severe anxiety, estrangement, and detachment. As the veteran builds a trusting and confident relationship with the horse, that trust begins to spill over into day-to-day interactions and to impact family relationships.

"I want to encourage all veterans having readjustment problems to try horseback riding," said Kendal.

Enrolling Larry in the equestrian therapy program proved pivotal in helping his other therapeutic programs become more effective. As Larry looked out over the open land, the horses and the vets mingling in quietude, he softly remarked, "Getting analyzed, counseled, and medicated can be important . . . but this is something that gives us a real, hands-on approach to getting our lives back."

His face was awash in hope.

But there was a glint in his eye as he took Kendal's hand, and a look of understanding passed between them. Larry may have found more ways to channel his warrior energy, but that doesn't mean there isn't the occasional high-energy bondage scene in their bedroom.

* * *

Although Kendal felt a little ashamed sharing details of her sex life with the group at SPA Day, she was unspeakably relieved to discover that she wasn't alone. Other women shared stories about how the excitement of aggressive sex evolved into the couples enjoying experimental sex and a lust for adventure. A few spoke about how this intensity sometimes bordered on physical abuse, and the women discussed the fine line: If she doesn't get anything out of it and is just a receptacle, it's rape. But if she enjoys it, it's just a different kind of intimacy—one that can be a healthy release, so long as lines of communication remain open.

Talking about sex is seldom easy, and can be even more upsetting when one partner is hurt, disabled, and suffering. Hopefully, sharing these stories will help other women feel less alone, and also educate them about what's healthy play and what's borderline abuse. Sex is an important part of the marriage relationship, and it can be terrifying to believe that you'll never be intimate with your partner again in the way you'd like. But as Kelly's and Kendal's stories prove, sometimes a tumultuous journey can lead to a satisfying ending.

CHAPTER 6

STAY OR GO?

*One of the things about equality is not just that you be
treated equally to a man, but that you treat yourself
equally to the way you treat a man.*

—MARLO THOMAS

"SHOULD I STAY or should I go? The question haunted
me," said Amy, her voice catching in her throat. "I didn't want
to end my marriage; I just wanted to stop hurting. I made lists
and prayed, but the answers never came."

She went on, listing the painful questions that so many
women with badly injured spouses have asked themselves: Will
my child hate me if I leave my husband? Won't he resent me
for leaving his father and the life they know? Even when he's
grown, will he still hate me for leaving his poor disabled dad? Is
it fair to stay with my husband out of pity? Doesn't he deserve
to be loved? Is it better to have my husband than no one at all?
How will I make it financially on my own? What will God, our

parents, society, and our friends think of me for leaving my injured husband? Will I go to hell?

"I spent a long time stuck in indecision," she admitted. "I was so scared, because I knew this would be the most difficult choice of my life. But at least I was willing to look at my options." Amy's story follows in this chapter, and we learn the path she takes.

These women pour their hearts and souls into their spouses' recoveries, endlessly and selflessly. They put up with fatigue, stress, and confusion, often becoming the only person holding their families together. They are mothers, lovers, fighters, and sages all day, every day.

But although wounded warriors' wives should be celebrated for their dedication and endurance, they should also be recognized as human beings with frailties, faults, needs, and breaking points. The majority of this book is written about the wives who stay, who grit their teeth through the nightmares and surgeries and endless bureaucratic BS. But it's vital that we also explore the flip side: the wives who leave. Not every marriage survives the trials of PTS and disability; not every wife can reconfigure her entire life to accommodate a wounded spouse. Those who stick it out are definitely heroes, but that doesn't mean those who leave are villains.

Mary, whose story follows, understands the urge to leave. "One night my husband woke up, or I woke up, and he was on top of me, strangling me. And I was trying to wake him up and going, 'John, John, wake up. Wake up!' He was thrashing around in bed in a blind panic, soaked in sweat, with his heart pounding and his hands around my throat. And he finally looks at me and says, 'What?' I'm like, 'You're strangling me.' He went, 'No, I'm not.' He woke up flooded with fear and told me his nightmares were about explosions, victims crying out for help, his friends being shot, and loud, frightening blasts."

Other women told how they guided husbands suffering from flashbacks out of the nightmares and into the present. They tried to a figure out a way to wake them up without touching them, so their loved ones wouldn't respond as though they were being attacked. The women talked about playing uplifting music for their spouses, listening as their husbands described their nightmares to help them work through the trauma, and keeping them away from experiences that triggered flashbacks. The women agreed that sometimes hearing from someone who truly, personally understands what they have been through is all it takes to rekindle hope.

Sometimes, however, it takes more than this, and sometimes a couple never finds a way to bring that hope back to life. According to Pentagon data, more than 30,000 military marriages ended in divorce in fiscal 2011, up from 27,000 in 2004. Although the military divorce rate has fluctuated somewhat, it is still quite high. Marriage is challenging enough when both spouses are healthy and happy, and can become impossible when trauma and injury are in the mix.

* * *

In many cases, the inability to practice self-care pushes wives over the edge. When every waking moment is spent tending to someone else's needs, these wives' own needs become neglected. And if they *stay* neglected, things tend to fall apart.

The happiest married couple I've worked with as a physical therapist had an interesting little routine. The patient's wife would often be a half hour late to pick him up from physical therapy, because she'd go and get a manicure during his appointment. He'd had an arm and a leg amputated, and had to lie on the physical therapy mat after our treatment was done, waiting for her to return. At first when she did this, he was livid, but he got over it when he saw this well-groomed, smiling, confident woman walk through the door. She showed up happy, rested, and ready to give him 100 percent of her energy and time. She *never* played the martyr, which helped them keep their sense of humor and love alive. Her actions might have seemed selfish on the surface, but since she knew how to take care of herself, she was able to take care of her husband and encourage him positively through his rehab. She never played the mother role, never nagged him, but instead remained his lover, partner, and most ardent cheerleader.

I left my marriage because, for too many years, I didn't practice self-care. I let my career, my passions, and my health slide during my marriage, and I ended up blaming my husband for my unhappiness and destroying our marriage through an affair. I don't want to see the wives I meet at SPA Day do the same, so I encourage them to practice healthy self-care. As I share what I've learned, I do my best to convince them that they must take time to refuel, whether they stay in a stressful marriage or find that they must leave.

Many full-time caregivers say that they feel like enlisted soldiers themselves—but without the structure, the camaraderie, and the institutional support that real soldiers have. Many of them find that counseling is available for their husbands' PTS, but not for their own stress or the anger, fear, and guilt that often haunt their own nightmares. The wounded receive Purple Heart medals and are seen as heroes. Too often, the caregivers stand in the shadows, unacknowledged and underappreciated, which can cause resentments to build up.

"I am not only my husband's caregiver, nonmedical attendant, appointment scheduler, cook, driver, and groomer, but I am also his loving wife, faced with my own stresses and frustrations," Carla said. "What is upsetting is the lack of support, compassion, and benefits for caregivers. Helping him through his treatment is what I want to do. But I need the system to help me do that."

After a long legislative struggle, in 2013 the VA began to officially recognize, train, and pay small stipends to family caregivers. According to the VA, certified caregivers will now have access to their own mental health services and paid vacation.

Most of these women are trying to emerge from the narrow role of caregiver and embrace other identities too. One woman told me, "We both needed him to start caring for himself. I needed to quit being the one who kept track of every tiny detail. It was hard for both of us to let go."

That "letting go" can mean the difference between saving an ailing marriage and needing to walk away. In either situation, self-care is essential. The following are stories from Amy and Mary, both of whom have grappled with the question of leaving or staying and have dealt with the guilt, shame, and anguish involved when such a painful decision must be made.

AMY: THE GUILT OF GOING

Walking away from your partner can feel like a profound betrayal, but sometimes it's the only choice that remains. That was the case for Amy.

Amy and Jeff met at college in Texas in 2005, married early, and had a son together. Jeff was a sandy-haired young man with a charming splash of freckles across his face, who admitted that he'd had a crush on Amy for six months before he worked up the guts to ask her out. Amy fell hard for him and allowed their relationship to move quickly, following her heart and eagerly diving into domestic life. They married, and within a few months, Amy was pregnant. A year later, when Jeff decided to abandon his degree to join the Army, Amy supported him, though she did worry about the challenges this decision would bring into their lives. She worked as a middle-school teacher on and off, and was forced to juggle her job and taking care of their infant son when Jeff was deployed to Iraq for the first time in 2007.

In February 2009, during his second deployment, Jeff was leading a patrol when an IED exploded nearby, killing three of his men and gravely wounding him. The blast broke his spine and left leg and caused many internal injuries, including TBI. He was in such bad shape that the doctors didn't expect him to pull through. He surprised everyone when he did, but he was a changed man. Jeff was flown home relatively quickly and went through round after round of surgeries as the medical teams attempted to piece him back together. Amy was distraught, barely able to sleep, and her hair began to thin due to the stress of worrying about her husband, caring for her son, and attempting to keep the family financially stable. What's more, the surgeries didn't seem to help much. Even after months of recovery and rehab, Jeff couldn't walk, speak clearly, use the bathroom, or eat on his own. He needed care and help around the clock—all day, every day. Naturally, those tasks fell to his wife.

Physical therapy and rehab continued for years after he came home, but even with payouts from insurance and the Army, money became tight. When she looked in the mirror, Amy felt as if she'd aged a decade in just a few years. In the spring of 2013, Amy and Jeff had been married for eight years. And after spending the last four of those years caring for Jeff *and* their son full-time, Amy took her son and walked out, discussing her decision with no one.

"I hated myself for it, but I just couldn't stay," she told the other wives at SPA Day. "I was exhausted and overwhelmed and starting to become useless as a mother to my son. I couldn't work, we had almost no money, and my entire life had become about Jeff's recovery."

Amy told me that she hardly recognized her husband in the man who returned from Iraq, and eventually she couldn't even recognize herself.

"I felt lost and alone. Jeff's mother helped out as much as she could, but she didn't really understand what it was like to be me," she explained. "I knew we'd never have sex again because of his injuries, so I stopped taking care of myself, my hair, putting on makeup. I was strung out and tired all the time. When I nearly fell asleep while driving home from the grocery store, that was the last straw."

"Gabe was affected, too. He was only two when his dad left for the first time, and nearly five when his dad came back to us broken. Gabe was scared and confused; he started to wet the bed and stopped talking to his friends. Both of us were a mess, and I felt like I had to leave to save us." When Amy spoke about her choice, it was clear she still hurt, even three years later.

She took a small amount of solace from Jeff's family's reaction. She knew that they were still upset and felt betrayed by her, but they weren't cruel about it.

"About a year after I left, I ran into Jeff's mom at the grocery store. She was tense, but she seemed to understand a bit," Amy said. "She told me, 'You went through hell. I still think you should have stayed, but I know it was so, so hard for you and Gabe.'"

Amy told us that Jeff's mother is his primary caretaker now, and he has moved into a new house, which has been fitted with ramps and special equipment for his needs. Because of a long and complex custody battle, neither Jeff nor his mom have seen much of Gabe since Amy left. Although she doesn't want to cut her son off from his father, she's just not sure how to manage the relationship with custody in dispute.

"I know I hurt everyone when I left. I may never get over that," Amy told us, her voice cracking a bit. "But I was drowning. If I hadn't left, I'm not sure I would've been able to keep going. I was having some pretty dark thoughts."

Amy and Gabe moved a couple of towns away from Jeff, but she can't quite fathom moving farther. Amy knows that the custody fight will end eventually, and doesn't want to deprive Jeff of any contact with his growing son. She hasn't dated much since she left, which she attributes partially to her lingering guilt and partially to an overbooked life of teaching, raising her son, and doing her best to stay fit and healthy.

"Sometimes I wonder if I'll ever really move on. I may have gotten out physically, but part of me is still trapped in that house with him."

When one spouse is injured—and especially if the injury is a brain injury—statistics show that the couple is highly likely to separate. Those who don't separate nearly always go through periods of extreme stress, depression, and fighting, as the stories in previous chapters have shown. Caring for a wounded warrior is hard, which is why the women who stay deserve praise and admiration. But it also means that some wives will leave, and that often they have good reasons for doing so. Even if it is a painful decision, sometimes leaving is necessary for the sake of one's own survival.

MARY: OPTIONS

One hot September night in 2015, Mary sat down at the kitchen table and rubbed at her watery green eyes. It was time to face some hard facts, and she was steeling herself for making even harder decisions.

She admitted to herself that John almost never opened up to her anymore, and when he did, it was only because he was drunk. She felt disconnected and abandoned by him, and was finally beginning to understand that if she wanted change, she'd have to make it herself. As she sat there asking herself if she should stay in this marriage or let it go, she remembered the man she had married. Back then, John had been silly and kind, strong and fit. Her Marine. She could still see his young face in her mind's eye, just twenty years old.

Truth be told, Mary had already lived a lifetime by the time she met John in 2007. At nineteen, she was the single mother of a one-year-old boy. Mary's first husband simply walked out the door when their son was just ten months old and never came back, leaving Mary scrambling to create a stable life for herself and her child. When she met John two years later, John immediately connected with her son, and the three became a family quickly and easily. They married in 2009, and John adopted her son as his own. Mary saw him as her knight in shining armor.

Three years into their happy marriage, John was deployed to Afghanistan. There, as he traveled in a desert convoy, an IED hit his tank, causing injuries to his hip, knee, and head. Nine months after he'd sustained the injuries, he was finally well enough to return home.

Reunited with his family, John told Mary that he wanted to become a full-time student. He was granted a full medical discharge in 2013. He was still mobile despite his injuries, and eager to move on to the next phase of his life. Mary had a college degree in child development and agreed to support the family by teaching prenatal health care. She didn't mind being financially responsible for her husband and son. She was just glad to have her man home and her family back together, looking toward what appeared to be a bright future.

But life in her home was not as it had been before he left. When Mary had a hard day at work, John couldn't empathize or even converse. Day after day, he sat stone-faced in his chair in the living room, unable to talk to his wife, unable to connect with his seven-year-old son. Mary could tell that he was haunted by memories, that part of him was stuck in a painful, traumatic, and private place.

"It didn't take much to remind John of Afghanistan," Mary recalled. "And when he remembered, he didn't feel like going out and pretending to be happy."

Mary asked him to tell her what had happened back there, but John just grunted and shuffled off to the fridge for a beer. Alcohol was quickly becoming his crutch. During the week, he buried himself in schoolwork, but on the weekends John dove into row upon row of beers. Sometimes he would down a half dozen cans and yell, "I just want to be alone. Leave me alone!"

Mary tried to tell herself that this was not John shutting her out; this was just John coping to the best of his ability. And at times, that rationale worked. After all, she didn't fully understand what he had faced during wartime. Who was she to judge?

When Mary began to talk to other wives and do some research, she learned that this behavior was common among combat veterans. She began to understand that when John had been in Afghanistan, he'd simply had to turn off his emotions. And it wasn't just a matter of the experience being personally confusing; letting his emotions flow freely while in combat could have been life-threatening. He would have been less able to give and take directions, and it would have been more difficult for him to react swiftly in a crisis.

With more research, Mary learned that John was experiencing a "deadening of emotions" or "emotional or psychic numbing."

Mary found some comfort in the thought that maybe John was just in a stage—the numbing stage—and that someday the stage would end.

When she sought help from friends and relatives, she got well-meaning but unhelpful advice like, "Keep working on it" or "Let me talk to him." Some were less caring and more judgmental, saying, "If you haven't made any progress, you're not doing it right. You're not trying hard enough." That was Mary's deepest fear. What *was* doing it right? What *was* enough? Was she failing her husband and her marriage?

After a horrible night of nightmares, she approached John about seeking help. That terrible flashback was his way to confront or cope with the traumatic events he had experienced in combat. Mary begged him to go with her to see a therapist who could guide them through this confusing maze.

"It's not a good idea, Mary. A jihadist disguised himself as a guard at our base and then turned his weapon on my comrades. Nothing can erase that memory," he told her.

"John, I think we have to do something different from what we have been doing," she said. "We're all in a lot of pain, and we need to talk to an expert. I didn't even know you shared a base with Afghan soldiers. You must have wondered what other Afghan soldiers were the enemy."

"So we go get help and then what? Then everyone thinks I'm a pussy?"

"Going to see a therapist doesn't make you a pussy," she insisted.

"We do that, we walk in those doors, and they never see me the same way again," he said. "I'm the weak one, the crazy one— the one that doesn't get promoted. You don't understand the culture. I've lived it."

Mary pushed a bit more, hoping for a breakthrough, but John just turned to her and said, "I've got this. I can handle it in my own way, in my own time."

For a few weeks after she proposed they consult a therapist, she noticed a sort of reprieve. John was a bit softer, easier to talk to, and seemed less tortured. But about a month later, Mary came home to a plastered husband. John was drunker than she'd ever seen him.

She told their eight-year-old son to go to his room.

"What's going on?" she asked her husband.

For the first time in a long time, Mary saw something human and fragile behind her husband's eyes.

"Mary, it's just . . . you wouldn't believe what I've seen," he said. "These people were merciless."

Mary held John's hand, and he told her about how the Afghan insurgent who John had thought was a guard on the base, protecting them, killed his friends. This Afghan soldier had full access to the base, as he was being trained to protect his own country, but he turned on his trainers and murdered John's buddies. As hard as it was to hear these things, Mary was grateful that he was finally talking about what was haunting him. He spoke, she listened, and she felt they might be reforging their former bond.

The next day Mary brought up therapy once more, and was crushed when John refused again. He trusted no one and continued to believe that admitting he needed help was a sign of weakness. As the days went on, Mary realized that John was angry with her. He looked at her as if she were a stranger, rather than the wife who had faithfully stood by him throughout his seven-year military career. He began to check her phone daily, convinced she was having an affair. His mistrust of the world had spilled over onto her.

Mary tried reaching out to one of John's best friends from his unit to discuss John's struggles, but he wasn't much help. He told Mary that John had mentioned VA representatives reaching out a few months earlier, but that he'd refused to take any help. He said that yes, if John decided to seek counseling it would be confidential, but he knew from his own experiences with the VA system that John needed to make his own medical appointments. There was help for the nightmares. He had to work through this memory with a therapist.

When John had been medically discharged from the Marines, shortly after his return from Afghanistan, Mary thought it might have a positive impact on their lives, but John's symptoms only became more severe. Emotionless, unresponsive, and unavailable, he became what she called an "ice man." She wasn't sure if she could live like that anymore. Even if John wouldn't seek help, she knew she had to get it together for herself and her son.

Mary signed up for the Operation Family Caregiver program and for private counseling. She found further support when she attended SPA Day, where she met other wives of wounded warriors.

"I was sad to hear other women's stories, but I felt a piece of myself in each story I heard," she said. "There was a part of my life in these women's stories, and I no longer felt alone."

Fueled by a stronger sense of purpose, Mary went home from SPA Day ready to talk to her husband, to share with him all of her new insights. She wanted to tell him that they weren't alone, that others were experiencing the same thing. But when she arrived home, she found out that John was "not alone" in a very different way.

John confessed that he had been seeing another woman.

On that long, hot September night, Mary faced the decision to stay or go, and she thought long and hard about her journey. She was a different woman than the one who'd met John as a young, scared single mom. She was financially responsible, a strong mother, and she knew who she was at her core. She knew that she hadn't caused John's trauma, that she couldn't control his recovery, and that she couldn't cure him.

Realizing the gravity of the situation, she was hit hard with a profound sense of abandonment. All this time, she'd told herself that he wasn't shutting her out, wasn't turning away from her. And yet he was; he was turning to another woman. John's head and heart were no longer linked to Mary or her son.

She reflected back on her last therapy session, when she had complained about John being emotionally numb. The therapist had pointed out that over the years, she herself had become numb. When Mary had first researched John's PTS symptoms, she'd read that wives and children of combat veterans also experience numbness at first, too. But this wasn't just a phase. Just like John, she was afraid of the feelings inside her, afraid to face the years of pent-up anger, hurt, and a sense of loss. She couldn't handle comparing what she'd hoped her marriage would be to what her marriage had actually become.

Then she felt the stinging blow—the ultimate fear in her heart—that her son might never have another father figure. A sob emerged from deep inside of her, and for a moment it hurt so badly that she prayed for the emotional numbness to return; she wanted to feel nothing. But at that moment she saw her son's face as he came down the stairs. He had the same look in his eyes that she had become used to seeing in the mirror: war-weary, afraid, never knowing what was about to come.

That's when the clarity came. Mary knew what she could and could not live with. John in emotional trouble, John with PTS and combat fatigue, John with a drinking problem—all of those were difficult, but she could brave them. Not this, though—not this complete and total abandonment. Suddenly, she was grateful that she could feel the pain. Because when she felt it, she was able to see that they weren't a family, and that they hadn't been for a long, long time. And in that moment, Mary realized it was time to go.

Instead of fear, she felt her heart surge with hope. She knew that it was going to be difficult, but she also knew it was going to be okay, because deep down *she* was okay. Somewhere along the way she had learned to become her own hero. She stood up from the table and headed upstairs to throw a few essentials in a suitcase. Then she wiped away one last tear, grabbed her son's hand, and they walked out the door.

* * *

The issue of staying or leaving is fraught with indecision for these women. Even if a wife is unhappy in her marriage, she might be reluctant to give up on her man, especially if he has come home with serious injuries or has yet to seek help. Fear of the unknown and of loneliness also play a role, as do fears surrounding emotional and financial hardships that might arise after separation. Women who were abused as children often stay because of unconscious patterns learned in childhood. Others fear that no one else will ever love them, and if they've put on weight or let themselves go, they can feel trapped by the looming possibility of lifelong loneliness. Staying can feel overwhelming and terrifying, but sometimes that seems preferable to diving alone into uncharted waters.

Wives also might worry that their decisions will result in negative psychological effects for their husbands and children. If a woman's husband is suicidal or extremely dependent on her, she might fear that he'll deteriorate significantly without her. If he has been violent, she might fear that he will lash out to hurt her, her children, himself, or even strangers. Wives in this situation who consider separation or divorce sometimes offer an ultimatum: seek treatment for your PTS, alcoholism, or drug addiction, or I walk. When this doesn't work, it can be devastating, leaving the wife to ask herself, "If he won't help himself, how can I?"

Both staying and leaving involve risk and pain.

We'd like to think that we welcome these injured soldiers home with open arms; we are certainly providing more resources and support to our fighting men than we did after Vietnam. But these wars have dragged on for more than fourteen years, and the public's focus has shifted. There hasn't been a ticker-tape parade or treaty signing—a clear end—that forces us to reflect on the lives of disabled soldiers. As a society, do we take any responsibility to care for injured warriors, or is it all on their families? These brave men face multiple deployments over multiple years, stepping up so others don't have to serve. Is it fair that this tiny percentage of men does all the fighting? Or that after the ceremonies have been held and medals handed out, their lives and well-being fade from view?

Many wives of wounded warriors know that their husbands feel abandoned and betrayed by the country they served. This awareness can make leaving harder, even if the marriage has become terrifying or volatile. Some wives fear adding to their husbands' emotional burdens by deserting them.

But some marriages do dissolve. Some wives do leave. They do so weighed down with guilt and fear and doubt, but they do so to save themselves and their children. They leave because they need a fresh start and think their husbands might secretly want the same. The women who stay show bravery by turning their lives upside down and inside out to care for and support their wounded husbands. The women who leave show bravery by facing scorn and ridicule, fear and uncertainty, to do what they feel is right. Leaving behind a wounded warrior can be the hardest thing a wife will do in her entire life.

CHAPTER 7

NOT JUST SURVIVING BUT THRIVING: POSTTRAUMATIC GROWTH

Learning to be resilient and live with the memories goes on, demanding daily attention to wounds that never truly heal.

—LARRY M. EDWARDS

AFTER SERIOUS TRAUMAS, many wives of wounded warriors must dig deep to discover how the power of their own resilience can make their lives more meaningful. The military might call these women "dependents," but their husbands depend on them for the care they need to heal. When their husbands were wounded, they were wounded too.

Those that undergo posttraumatic growth (PTG) find that recovering from disaster may bring unexpected gifts. They discover new strengths and a deepened sense of purpose. They feel open to new experiences, their relationships improve, and their personal weaknesses transform into strengths. The paradox of loss is that sometimes a great deal can be gained.

This revelation was something that nearly all of the women who attended SPA Day shared with me.

"My attitudes and values have changed," Kelly said. "I'm more sensitive and caring. I concentrate more on being a human *being*, not a human *doing*."

"I've learned to be more patient and to slow down," Kendal told me. "I feel once you know people's problems, you can understand their needs and you are more sympathetic to those needs."

Katy said she felt like she'd undergone a transformation. "I wonder if I'm the same person I used to be. I feel more compassionate, more aware," she explained. "I have learned that people want to maintain their dignity, regardless of the problems they are facing, whether they are physical or mental. I think I have more of a sense of humor, and feel able to weed out trivial things."

"My whole concept of a fulfilling life has changed. I'm not what happened to me, but what I chose to become," Suzie said. "I can now enjoy the process and care from a distance, letting my husband heal at his own pace. I let my children learn from their mistakes without overcontrolling and playing God. I've stopped trying to fix everyone."

Jane explained that she views her new life with her husband as a second chance. "The daily reality has taught me to be grateful for the small things in life," she said. "Like the smile on my husband's face, enjoying coffee in the morning, and snuggling in bed with him. I no longer take these things for granted."

Jane has noticed remarkable changes in her own personality, too. "I've learned to be an advocate for my husband. I used to be quiet, shy, and polite, but now I stand up for his rights and ask lots of questions. This carries over to other areas of my life. I'm more of a participant and don't sit back and play the victim. I've learned when a challenge presents itself I can handle it by breaking it down into manageable goals. 'What can I do about it today?' I've learned empowerment. Now I'm a professional no matter what situation I find myself in."

The women talked about how new traits—including compassion, advocacy, and empathy—had bloomed within them, and swapped stories about how passion and humor had come to their rescue in some situations. All of these qualities can develop as part of PTG. With all of the information-seeking these women must do to ensure their husbands get the care and treatment they deserve, they learn to be extroverted and charismatic. Wounded warriors are often unwilling to ask for help out of stubborn pride, so their spouses must step up, getting what their families need using a combination of determination and charm. As the old adage goes, "You catch more flies with honey than with vinegar." These women—who have learned how to be diplomatic but persistent, friendly but unyielding—are living proof that the adage is true.

Remember the wife who brought weekly boxes of candy for the nurses? They never forgot her, and certainly never neglected her husband's treatments. It's true that the squeaky wheel gets the grease, especially at crowded, understaffed hospitals. If a wife is sitting by her husband's bedside chatting up the doctors, therapists, and nurses, her husband is more likely to get better care. Many wives of wounded warriors know that, and wisely use it to their advantage.

During PTG, submissive women become assertive, quiet women become talkative, doormats become powerhouses. These women are able to recognize the new challenges their lives now present and rise to meet them. No one wants trauma or pain or disability to enter their lives, but some people are able to harness that hurt and use it for important personal growth. It's a testament to human resilience that such a dark experience can end up having a silver lining.

"I didn't know I had it in me" is a refrain I've heard over and over again. I've seen some warriors' wives exploit the system to get benefits when their husbands weren't hurt, but they were the exception, not the rule. I've met many, many *more* women with injured husbands who have stepped up to challenges on the home-front battlefield with flexibility and resourcefulness. When red tape threw up roadblocks, giving in was not an option for them.

When I met Mai at SPA Day, she was bubbly, friendly, warm, and chatty. We clicked immediately, and she opened up to me right away, making it clear that she'd experienced a powerful transformation through PTG. She told me that in high school she was a shy girl, never speaking up in class or going out with big groups of friends, and she certainly was not the popular cheerleader type. She remained fairly quiet and introverted for most of her adult life, too, including the first part of her marriage. But when her husband came home from deployment needing care, Mai discovered that she had to change in order to take on her new role. She set her mind to cultivating the skills she needed to secure resources for her husband and family. She forced herself outside her comfort zone so that she could become the powerhouse in her marriage. She transformed her shyness into strength.

Mai now helps others find the resources they need, giving her life new meaning as a speaker, teacher, and caretaker for wounded warriors. At all of our SPA Days, she stands up to share her story and speaks with authority about all the resources she's discovered and the ones she's created. She gives and shares because she has been through the trials herself, and other women flock to her for advice. Her hard-earned charisma makes people want to get to know her, hear her story, and stay connected to her.

Read on to get to know Mai better and to hear about how caring for her wounded husband has transformed her life for the better. You'll also hear from Natasha and Jenny, who experienced PTG in amazing ways and have generously shared their stories with me.

MAI: MAKING MARGARITAS OUT OF LEMONADE

For months following his return from Iraq, Mai's husband, Lanh, slept on their floor. He had injured his back while extracting a pilot from a grenade-riddled aircraft in Iraq, fracturing his thoracic vertebra, severing his spinal cord, and leaving him paraplegic. This violent incident occurred just one month after he'd recovered from an IED explosion in 2010, and he also incurred painful burns and gunshot wounds during the rescue. His back hurt so badly that even the firmest mattress was too soft for him. Knowing he was a softie at heart, Mai saw a touch of irony in his new need for hard surfaces.

Born in Saigon and raised in Los Angeles, California, Lanh had enlisted in the Army at the age of twenty in the aftermath of 9/11. He chose to become an aircraft rescue firefighter, and he was absolutely fearless—no matter how terrifying a crash site might look, he dove in to save his fellow soldiers without a second thought. After multiple harrowing deployments and a decade of hard work, he returned to Fort Lewis near Tacoma, Washington, in 2011, with not one but two Purple Heart medals and a medical discharge.

Mai met Lanh shortly after his return, and she became his wife and best advocate. She was a painfully shy, soft-spoken, petite woman with fine features and stick-straight hair, but he brought out her playful spirit. Even while he was dealing with illness and disability, Lanh was a tireless flirt, and Mai couldn't resist his charms.

The couple married and did their best to build a life in Washington. Lanh received a fantastic job offer with the local fire department, but he found he couldn't handle the physical demands of the job. Not being able to provide for his family overwhelmed him, leaving him not only physically but also mentally and emotionally crushed. The discrepancy between a fighting spirit and a body that could no longer answer the call caused him a great deal of anguish.

"When your spouse's identity is a military warrior," Mai said, "being forced into civilian life is a tough battle. Even with his injuries, Lanh wanted to serve and fight for his country. He said if he wasn't physically hurt, he would go back tomorrow."

He also worried about providing. Lanh was grateful for the recognition he'd received for his service and sacrifice, but Purple Hearts cannot feed and house people. Mai thought that it might help to move back to California, where Lanh would be closer to his family.

Relocating was the first big decision they made on their own after Lanh left the Army. After a stressful but successful move in 2013, the young couple found themselves in Southern California in an unfurnished house, with their two-year-old son and little else. The lack of furniture didn't faze Lanh—his spinal injuries were so severe that sleeping on a mattress was more likely to cause agonizing pain than grant him a night of rest. And he was delighted to be closer to his hometown and family.

Mai, on the other hand, felt desperate upon their arrival. They lacked even the bare essentials for their home, such as a refrigerator. But purchasing appliances and furnishings would have to wait until she could find a job that allowed for flexible scheduling. In Washington, she'd been working as a nursing assistant for the elderly. But since Lanh's extensive injuries meant he needed near-constant monitoring and help, she'd had to quit her job to serve as his caregiver.

As a nursing assistant, Mai had learned that simple kindness could go a long way toward encouraging patients to become independent, and she used that tool in caring for Lanh. But her shyness, which had persisted since high school, held her back from getting the help *she* needed. When a friend of the family told her about Patriots and Paws, a nonprofit organization that provided furniture and other necessities for veterans who needed help getting back on their feet, Mai was reluctant to make the call. Finally, she reasoned that this wasn't about her—it was about her family. Being married to a man who had come home wounded brought out both her maternal and warrior instincts.

She made the call, and the organization arranged for a refrigerator to be delivered to her apartment. While she was on the line, the director of the program asked if Mai needed a mattress.

"That's probably not going to work," Mai told him.

She told the director how Lanh's injuries prevented him from sleeping on most mattresses. Hearing that detail, the organization offered to supply the couple with a special double-reinforced mattress that had extra bracings to hold its shape, so that they could finally sleep together again. The bed and the refrigerator—plus a couch, a dresser, and even a piano—that the couple received from Patriots and Paws helped them turn the blank-slate apartment into a space that felt like their own.

"We asked for one thing," Mai said, "and got a whole bunch." None of this would have happened if Mai hadn't overcome her shyness.

Mai was amazed by how quickly their apartment began to feel like home. Since she had a second son on the way, she was especially grateful that they could put what resources they did have toward a room for the baby.

"We would have furnished his room first, and I'm sure it would have taken a full year to get everything else for the apartment," she said.

After moving to Southern California, they also found a helpful VA counselor. Lanh's family was also a great support system. It was difficult for Mai to leave her own family in Washington, but the move forced her to become more independent.

"Moving was scary," Mai said, "but all the positive changes in our lives stem from taking that one big leap of faith."

It didn't happen overnight, but as Lanh got stronger, the couple got stronger, too.

Mai advised the other wives at SPA Day, "Brace yourself

with a dependable network of family, friends, and professionals to catch you if you fall."

In early 2015, Lanh found a desk job at the local fire department, where he helped with fire prevention programming. He was thrilled to be able to work and bond with fellow firefighters again, and the energy in the firehouse kept his spirits high. Once he was working, the couple was able to donate the furniture they had received back to Patriots and Paws. They never treated the furniture as a gift, but rather as a loan that helped them get back on their feet. They gave it back so that other veterans could receive it, use it, and benefit from the organization's generosity.

Even more gratifying was being able to own a home of their own. A few years back, Lanh's social worker had told them about a program called Operation Homefront that helped veterans apply to live mortgage-free. Lanh was against it, initially. He felt they'd already received so much, and there were others who were much worse off. But overcoming her shyness and seeing the results of her newfound confidence paid off, and Mai didn't back down.

"It took a year and a half to convince him to apply," she said.

Her persistence was rewarded when, during the Fourth of July weekend in 2015, at a ceremony attended by Tim McGraw and sponsored by Chase bank and Operation Homefront, Lanh and Mai were presented with a new home.

"It was a wonderful and unexpected blessing. Some people say make lemonade out of lemons, but I say we made margaritas out of lemonade!" Mai said. "The lemonade was my husband coming home alive. In our new home we threw a party where we served margaritas, saying life is good, let's have a celebration and share."

Someday, Mai would like to go back to school so she can become a registered nurse, but right now her focus is on her family and helping fellow caregivers in the wounded warrior community. She has learned so much about the VA's health-care system and other resources available to veterans that she wants to reach out to other families and pass along helpful information so they know they aren't alone. She now posts daily on Facebook about resources for wives of wounded warriors, and she talks in person to those who need her help.

And that's something Mai never could have imagined doing before she met Lanh.

"When Lanh is in pain, my house is in pain," Mai said.

She couldn't make Lanh change, but by embracing uncertainty and facing the challenge of helping her husband reestablish himself, she has changed herself. She's become outgoing, someone who asks questions and finds answers. Mai's story illustrates how needing to protect one's family can be an opportunity to build personal strength.

When I met Mai at my foundation's SPA Day, she was so open and warm that I would never have guessed that she'd suffered from profound shyness in the past. Had I not known she was the wife of a wounded warrior, I would have assumed she was a spokeswoman for a charitable organization, not someone who'd been through the kind of hardships she and her husband had faced.

Mai told me, "At my first job as a nursing assistant, I was sweet and quiet, taking direction, but never leading. After Lanh came home injured, I had to tap into a strength I didn't know I had to get help for my husband and family."

An inspiration to her entire community, Mai recognizes that this tough journey has given her a deeper sense of meaning and mission. She's not just surviving; she is thriving. And her generosity and advocacy encourage others to follow in her footsteps. Her example shows us that sometimes what comes out of the ashes is better than what went down in flames.

NATASHA: A CONSTANTLY CHALLENGING
ENDEAVOR FUELS INNER FIRE

Natasha met Troy in 2003, while working at the front desk of the local YMCA. As she checked him in for his daily workouts, she couldn't stop herself from checking out his muscular physique. He could have passed for a pro basketball player, and he had the sweet, open face of a little boy. Soon loaded glances turned to flirting, flirting to dating, and dating to a love that grew fast and deep. While Natasha was only nineteen, Troy had already enlisted in the Air Force, so they fast-tracked their wedding, knowing that they would be partners for life. When Troy was sent overseas in the first year of their marriage, he and Natasha had already gotten a head start on building a family. They did their best to enjoy their time together at home when Troy was on leave, and shortly after their daughter Alisa was born, they decided to try for another baby. After their second daughter, Alex, came into their lives, the family felt complete—at least when all four of them were together.

Troy was away more than he was home, deployed to several locations in the Middle East, and Natasha couldn't help but worry about him. He managed several years without a scratch, but then his luck ran out in the spring of 2006.

During a firefight in Iraq, a bullet ricocheted and pierced Troy's neck, entering under his right cheek and exiting the left side of his fifth cervical vertebra. Medics kept him alive long enough to fly to a military hospital in Baghdad, where they were able to stabilize him relatively quickly. Within a matter of days, he was on his way back to America to recover at home.

"I first began to realize what we were up against the day Troy arrived at the Walter Reed Medical Center," Natasha told us. "It was five days after his injury, and I was frantic. The only information I had came from patchy cell-phone calls from officers and doctors in Iraq."

Natasha, a tall, athletic African-American woman with a dazzling smile, performed like a rock star as she dealt with the challenges of her husband's return and the repercussions of his injuries. She kept her emotional responses under control and drew on her inner strength, courage, and wit as she worked to stay on top of the situation.

"I was studying and caring for our toddlers, Alisa and Alex, near Edwards Air Force Base in California, where we lived. I had to figure out how to make up my classes, have my mom take the children, and arrange day care for them," she explained. Once she had her details squared away, she jumped on a plane to see Troy. Natasha's clearheaded, pragmatic actions ensured that her family moved toward a solution rather than further into a calamity.

"Something inside me just clicked, and I swung into action," she recalled. "I knew I needed to assess the situation and focus my energy on developing a strategy to manage it."

When Natasha arrived at the intensive care unit, she saw a series of monitors near the nurse's station. One, identified by Troy's Social Security number, glowed with an X-ray of a shattered skull. She took a deep breath and asked for the room number. A doctor grabbed her arm as she was en route to Troy's room, saying, "Ma'am, why don't you sit here first and let me brief you on his injuries?"

Natasha had no problem letting the doctor know nothing could stop her from seeing her husband. She wasn't intimidated by the doctor's warnings or her husband's injuries. She knew that nothing would comfort her husband more than her presence at his side.

She quickly countered the doctor's words. "I don't care how bad he looks. I've been waiting five days to see him, and I'm going to his room right now."

The doctor let go of her arm, and she rushed toward Troy's room. As she stepped through the doorway, she barely recognized him.

His head was swollen and covered with dried blood and rows of staples. He was hooked to machines and had a huge halo of metal bars around his head and neck to keep his vertebra from severing his spinal cord. She thought he looked like a robot.

"Troy, it's me," she said softly, trying not to cry. She told him to squeeze her hand if he knew who she was. His head didn't move, but he squeezed.

Their youngest daughter, Alex, was deaf, which meant Natasha was no stranger to helping loved ones with disabilities. In fact, learning about Helen Keller's teacher, Anne Sullivan, had inspired Natasha to study social work.

As the days and weeks passed with Troy recovering slowly in the hospital, Natasha learned the hard way that when it comes to keeping track of the particulars during a loved one's emergency, every detail counts.

"Nothing prepared me for all the paperwork, decisions, and medical jargon that came at me," she said. "I had no medical or legal training. I had to rely on my wits every single time I was asked to sign something."

As more time went by, she felt more confident. "I learned every aspect of Troy's care to the point that I could help him when nurses weren't available. I learned enough medical terms to talk knowledgeably with doctors."

She was also savvy enough to request a copy of every piece of paper added to Troy's medical record.

"When a new doctor or therapist came in asking Troy questions he'd answered a thousand times before, or couldn't answer at all," she said, "I pulled out my records and pointed straight to the information. His injury had left him with near-total amnesia and great difficulty speaking. I knew I needed to stay vigilant about Troy's care."

Vigilance wasn't the only resource she needed to tap. Soon she realized that perseverance and ingenuity would be necessary to make it through this jarring transition.

Just when Natasha had finally become familiar with all the details involved in Troy's care, he was transferred to a VA rehabilitation hospital in Palo Alto, California.

"We were flown in a military transport plane," Natasha recalled. "I had just gotten him settled into his new room at the VA when a nurse said, 'Visiting hours are from one to seven p.m.' I looked at her, surprised. 'I'm sorry, I'm not a visitor. I'm Troy's wife and have been at his bedside for the last month. He has amnesia. I assumed I'd be sleeping here until I can find housing.'"

"She just said, 'Ma'am, here's a list of nearby hotels you can try. And here's the paperwork for the Fisher House in Palo Alto.' As I left, I saw Troy's eyes widen with fear. I spent an anxious, stressful night with my toddlers."

The next day, Natasha found Troy in the same terrified state and tried a different approach. She paged the nurse and said, "I don't mean to be a nuisance, but there must be some way for me to stay with my husband. This is a whole new environment for him. I'm the only one he recognizes. What can I do?"

"You can visit during visiting hours," the nurse replied, adamant.

Then a neuropsychologist stepped in. "Ma'am," she said, and her voice sounded tired, as if she had a job to do and Natasha was making it harder, "this is your husband's rehabilitation, not yours. It would be better if you left the work to us. Think of him as being away on a deployment."

Since the medical staff showed no signs of yielding, Natasha was flooded with anger and disappointment. She knew that Troy was better *because* she had helped with his care.

Another look into Troy's frightened eyes showed her something else: a glimmer of fight, a glimpse of Troy the proud airman. Natasha thought about herself—an Air Force wife—and what that meant to her. She had already mastered the logistics of one hospital, and she could do it again. It was not the time to back down.

With a deep breath, Natasha asserted, "I am going to be by my husband's side. If you won't help me do that, I'll find someone who will."

And that's exactly what she did. Natasha got busy contacting the local Air Force Reserve unit, VIP hospital visitors, and congressional offices. She even signed up as a hospital volunteer, knowing that this would allow her unrestricted visiting hours. On top of all that, she helped the hospital raise money to build more housing for patients' loved ones.

She said, "In short, I became an advocate. I went to war with my family by my side."

Natasha's war was a ferocious one. She saw Troy through several more months of recovery at the VA, then brought him home in early 2007, independent but in a wheelchair as a quadriplegic.

Four years later at SPA day, recognizing that she needed more support, Natasha signed up for the Rosalynn Carter Institute's Operation Family Caregiver Program, and her caregiver coach walked her through each setback and challenge as it arose. Although she relied on family and friends to help with cooking, childcare, and chores, Natasha found ways to raise her daughters, care for her husband, *and* complete her degree, all while continuing to raise money and raise voices in the name of all wounded veterans.

Today, Troy continues his remarkable recovery, majoring in finance in hopes of becoming a financial consultant for other vets. Natasha, who channeled her experience into helping other disabled veterans, is a licensed marriage and family counselor for the VA. In addition to her admiration for Anne Sullivan, she names renowned scientist Stephen Hawking as an inspiration. Though severely physically disabled from amyotrophic lateral sclerosis (ALS)—a degenerative nerve disorder commonly known as Lou Gehrig's disease—he has contributed to advances in cosmology and theoretical physics for decades.

"He exemplifies what it means to have a meaningful life despite hardship," Natasha explained. "His memoir was amazing. In it, he wrote, 'Before my condition was diagnosed,

I had been very bored with life. There had not seemed to be anything worth doing.' How amazing is that? He took his disability as a challenge."

Natasha knows she cannot fight this war alone, and her call to others is powerful. "My message is simple. The warriors who come home will need more than slogans, more than bumper stickers and ribbon magnets on cars. They'll need resources to get the health care they need, support for family members taking part in that care, and a nation committed to seeing them through."

She knows that it will take coordinated effort from many organizations to truly improve the lives of wounded warriors. But Natasha continues to pour her heart and soul into helping her husband's healing comrades, and, much like Anne Sullivan, who was the caregiving lifeline for Helen Keller, she is undaunted by the scale of her undertaking. Pressing for better conditions and more support for returning veterans—a constantly challenging endeavor—is what fuels her bright inner fire.

JENNY: SILVER LININGS

Imagine being disabled at the age of twenty-five.

Jenny's wife Marsha has faced that reality since her last tour in Afghanistan, when her Humvee was hit with an IED. Tragically, five men died in her vehicle, along with everyone in the vehicle behind them. Marsha swiftly moved into action, pulling burning bodies out of the vehicles as she attempted to save lives, ignoring injuries she was hardly aware she'd sustained. She was already disabled, but her body didn't know it yet.

Marsha had joined the Marines in 2011, and after her third nine-month tour of duty, she was medically discharged in 2014. Back home in San Diego—injured by the blast and attempting to recover—she underwent multiple operations and struggled to cope with PTS, TBI, seizures, sleep apnea, and the challenges of three fractured limbs.

The amazing woman supporting this amazing woman was Jenny, a petite twenty-six-year-old with a big heart, lots of hustle, and a full plate. When Marsha woke up in the middle of the night screaming from a nightmare or had difficulty shaking off a particularly rough flashback, Jenny was there to soothe her. Their relationship became Marsha's soft place to land during bouts of depression. At times, Jenny wasn't sure how to help Marsha. She witnessed both the mourning and the rage and, for months on end, she couldn't understand the scope of the burden Marsha carried. But when Marsha attended a PTS camp with other Marines, she returned to Jenny feeling more prepared to share, and mustered the strength to tell her partner what had happened when that IED exploded.

"I felt that I should have done more. I should have been able to save someone," Marsha told her.

Jenny realized then that—on top of all her other physical and emotional injuries—Marsha was suffering from terrible survivor's guilt. As time passed, the burden of survival grew larger and heavier, until Marsha needed help working through it from professionals at camp before she could even begin sharing it with her wife.

Although Jenny hadn't gone to Afghanistan herself, she was still deeply scarred by the war. She learned that trauma is far-reaching, deeply impacting people who've never even put on a uniform. Marsha's health and state of mind affected every aspect of their shared daily life. Marsha struggled with seizures from her TBI, so she couldn't drive or be alone with their children, and during her first year back at home she couldn't work. With their daily routines turned upside down, Jenny was overwhelmed and felt like their life together was spinning out of control.

Then one day, Jenny saw a flyer for SPA Day in *Operation Homefront Magazine* and knew immediately the event could help her. She attended SPA Day in 2015, where she connected with other women dealing with similar challenges and met Lorie, the executive director of the Southern Caregiver Resource Center. Jenny and Lorie were kindred spirits and ended up having several deep, frank conversations.

Jenny confided to Lorie, "I have problems too, mainly pent-up anger from always having to be strong and responsible. I'm afraid that if someone puts their arms around me, I might start crying and never stop."

At Lorie's urging, Jenny enrolled in the resource center's six-month Operation Family Caregiver program, sponsored by the Rosalynn Carter Institute for Caregiving. Through the intensive weekly sessions, she learned how to make the problems of day-to-day life more tolerable and manageable. Jenny honed the skill of living life one minute at a time. This state of mind helped her create balance and resist letting her family slip into chaos.

One specific thing Jenny learned was that PTS is more than a list of symptoms—it's a cycle of behaviors. The veteran re-experiences the trauma inside her own head, then attempts to bury the memories and feelings associated with it. This cycle of re-experiencing and burying the trauma is repeated over and over and over. As more than one wife shared at SPA Day after opening up and sharing memories, their partners tended to suddenly withdraw, as if saying aloud the things in their minds was a kind of betrayal.

"I was so excited when Marsha opened up to me about Afghanistan," Jenny said. "I thought that finally we would be close again. She even told me that she had more to tell me. But instead, she just shut down—more so than ever. She wouldn't even tell me what she wanted for dinner, and didn't let me touch her for a week."

Jenny told the group at SPA Day that she hadn't been sure how to respond when Marsha shared her brutal memories. She asked the other women, "What did I do wrong? I didn't know exactly what to say when she told me about some of her firefights. I'm not a psychologist, but I thought I was sympathetic. Maybe I wasn't sympathetic enough. Did I turn her off somehow?"

Over time, Jenny learned she hadn't done anything wrong. Marsha simply did what all PTS survivors do: she shut down and withdrew to survive her overwhelming emotions. And although it was helpful to learn she wasn't to blame, Jenny also found out that whether they wanted to or not, she and Marsha both needed to learn how to handle their troubling emotions. Otherwise those emotions would come out in more destructive ways.

Through all the struggles and tears and rage and lessons, Jenny has had clear flashes of what she calls "silver lining sightings" that help her get through the rough patches. Here Jenny shares her silver lining sightings in hopes that others might have sightings of their own:

1. Remain optimistic that the human spirit will prevail.

With a plethora of injuries and the profusion of prescriptions to go with them, Marsha once fought an addiction to the pain meds the VA prescribed early in her recovery. But with some help and support, she overcame the dependence. Afterward, she took up alcohol to help herself cope. Jenny could see her partner spiraling downward into endless patterns of substance abuse, and she wasn't sure how to pull her out again.

Luckily, a friend suggested they check out Wave Academy, an organization that helps veterans grappling with PTS overcome depression, sleeplessness, and even suicidal thoughts through aquatic bodywork therapy. This innovative technique often leads wounded warriors to better sleep, less pain, and a more positive outlook on life.

Marsha was hesitant at first, but Jenny's relentless optimism about the program eventually convinced her to give it a try. The best part was that Wave Academy welcomed them both to participate in the program, and the experience transformed them.

"Before the therapy sessions, I couldn't get control of the way I was thinking and was filled with thoughts of suicide," Marsha confided to Jenny. "I couldn't get a handle on my depression, stress, anger, or fear. Wave Academy has been the most beneficial thing I've done for my recovery."

Jenny knew she had gotten stronger, too, having gone through the program with her partner. Even though there were days when she felt as if her best efforts fell short, she had faith she could address and handle whatever might come next.

"When Marsha went to PTS camp without me, she came home so much better. It was like she was now paddling with both oars in the water, but I only had one oar," Jenny explained. "I was going around in circles while she shoved off into recovery, navigating the waters ahead. When I found programs like Wave Academy that I could participate in too, that's when my healing really started."

2. Find peace in a plan.

When her life was particularly hectic, Jenny helped herself by planning what she could. She ordered a Life Alert button for Marsha to wear in case of seizures, a fail-safe that helped Jenny feel more secure when Marsha was alone at home and Jenny was at work. Jenny also did drills with the kids, so they felt prepared in case anything went wrong. Their eldest child learned how to help her other mom keep her head up and away from sharp objects during a seizure, as well as how to call for help and stay calm. Jenny made a point of talking with her sons so they felt they could be open with her about their questions or fears.

In addition, Jenny took advantage of support groups and any VA programs offered to the family. The Southern Caregiver Resource Center offered free respite care to fill in when Jenny's parents couldn't help. She applied to Hearts of Valor—a weeklong retreat that she'd heard about at SPA Day—and was accepted. This meant she had the chance to talk and share with other women, learn deep relaxation techniques, and get expert input on how to cope with her family's unique needs. Creating structure and educating herself helped Jenny find serenity in a chaotic existence.

3. Allow those who love you to lift you.

Jenny once held four jobs to address the family's financial stress, doing everything from being a licensed beautician to working as an X-ray tech. A mother since the age of sixteen, she'd taken on a lot of responsibility from a young age—but working to support the family financially, caring for Marsha, and handling childcare on her own was too much. Day care helped with the kids, but it was incredibly expensive. So Jenny's family volunteered to sit with Marsha and the kids on weekends so that Jenny could work.

Now she calls her parents on a daily basis and confesses that without them, there is no way she would have lasted this long. Her dad, mom, and sister have gone above and beyond for her family, and although the trauma interrupted their lives too, they help out with grace and generosity. Jenny's sons—now ages ten and three—also offer support in their own sweet way by helping around the house and caring for their other mom. (The three-year-old offers mostly cuddles.)

"No matter how strong and capable you think you are, you can't do this alone," Jenny advised. "The people who love you want to help you. Let them, and be grateful for their support and generosity."

4. Get inventive.

Before her wife's injuries, Jenny was able to find social companionship in all the usual outlets, the gym being one of her favorites. But now that her schedule no longer allows for much of a social life, she uses work to its full social capacity. Lunchroom talks and coffee breaks have a new significance, and while it's not exactly like happy hour, she still experiences social companionship. Jenny explains, "You learn to get creative when your options are limited."

5. Pay it forward.

Jenny understands that PTS symptoms are not signs of weakness or disorganization, but that her wife and other vets are responding to specific combat-related experiences. One treatment for PTS is to get away from it all and spend time in the peace and quiet of nature. During Marsha's third deployment in 2013, Jenny and the children purchased and moved to a pistachio orchard in Fallbrook, California. The serenity of living in the country helped create a nurturing and tranquil home for the whole family when Marsha returned home. But perhaps more importantly, the family has begun to invite other veterans and their families to the farm to pick pistachios. By offering other recovering warriors the chance to spend a day resting and relaxing, they help themselves and the community of wounded warriors.

6. Remember that making yourself a priority is a priority.

Over the years, Jenny found that staying healthy is essential to upholding her family in their tumultuous situation. She admitted to smoking pot and taking Xanax to help her relax when Marsha first returned, but she now uses nonchemical coping mechanisms. She indulges in and enjoys the "simple things," such as lighting scented candles, enjoying a hot shower, or soaking her feet. She makes time to de-stress at night by stretching before bed and keeps her body happy by eating healthy foods. She treats herself to an at-home manicure and pedicure once a month. As a caretaker, she understands the importance of self-care as a survival mechanism. If she's tapped out, she won't have the strength to help anyone else with their struggles.

Seeing Jenny taking care of herself, maintaining her independence through her career, and focusing on her own personal growth gave Marsha the strength and freedom to heal on her own terms. Instead of nagging Marsha and treating her like a helpless child, Jenny strove to treat her as an equal partner. This gave Marsha the dignity and confidence to navigate her own road to recovery. She stayed with counseling, the Wave Academy, and other programs offered to wounded warriors until she was off all medications and ready to attend school.

Through the GI Bill, Marsha received her degree in business in 2015 and began working toward making a successful transition back into the civilian world. She admitted to being a little apprehensive at first about the stigma some employers might have against hiring combat veterans. But she had plenty of experience dealing with discrimination as a gay woman, so she wasn't going to let this stop her from finding a satisfying career. Part of her personal growth journey was to let go of worry about an interviewer's possible bias in hiring. Some people might judge her because she's a plus-sized woman, because she's gay, or because she's a returning combat vet. But she learned that she could only control her own choices. This proved to be a successful attitude and led to her being hired by a top agricultural firm. Through this new career, she also learned how to build their family pistachio farm into a thriving side business.

Jenny and Marsha both found ways to get support, work through their challenges, and come out the other side stronger, happier, and more successful.

"I'd never say I'm grateful that Marsha was hurt, obviously," Jenny said, "but I know that we both healed stronger than we were before. We're different people now. Better people. And I can't help but feel grateful for that."

GRIEF GROWTH

Each one of these brave women who has shared her story has experienced PTG in a different way. Each one went on a unique journey through heartrending challenges and drew strength from what she learned. Although not all of them discussed it openly at SPA Day, they likely experienced and dealt with grief as they traveled along their paths. Grief presents itself in a very different form when someone is moving toward PTG. Maybe you've heard of the five stages of grief as defined by Elisabeth Kübler-Ross? It wasn't until I started working with the wives of wounded warriors that I learned from one of the women a new way to name the process: "Five Stages of Grief *Growth*."

Educating myself about these stages has helped me to better understand what the wives of wounded warriors are going through. It also has allowed me to help them work through whichever stage they find themselves in, gain some level of acceptance, and adjust to their new normal. In my own life, every challenge—from the death of my marriage to the death of my father—has brought new life and personal growth. I can understand how thinking of the journey in terms of stages could help anyone, even if they aren't going through a personal crisis at the moment. Each one of us knows someone who *is* in crisis, and mindfulness of how that crisis might affect our friends and loved ones makes us better, stronger, more compassionate people.

Here are the Five Stages of Grief *Growth*, how to recognize them, and how they might be beneficial:

Stage 1. Denial

When faced with true trauma, we often reject its existence to protect our minds from shock. This is a mental coping technique that serves as our first emotional line of defense. As a woman at SPA Day shared, "When my husband went in for his second surgery, we were in denial. We were numbed by the shock of having to endure another surgery that he might not make it through. We needed time to process this new assault."

Other feelings of denial include, *There's nothing wrong with me, I'm fine*, or, *This can't be happening. It's all some sort of mistake.* Denial is actually there to cushion the blow of a new reality. It allows us to navigate the fog so we can make it through the day. Others might think it's unhealthy at the time, but it's an important part of moving toward healing and growth. Let denial happen organically. It will burn itself out when the time is right.

Stage 2. Anger

After the numbness of denial wears off, we are faced with our harsh new reality, and the shock hits us full force. We might yearn deeply for the way things were, or wonder what we could have done differently. If we focus on the unfairness of our situation, rage floods our system. *Why me? I hate my life! I'm over this!* We are often told that anger is pointless, but in reality it is an important part of processing pain. Keeping anger bottled up always backfires, and feeling it is a natural, normal part of living through a life-altering trauma. Anger can even help create the motivation to ask more questions, change unfair situations, and advocate for yourself and your loved ones.

Stage 3. Bargaining

Anger takes a lot of energy and can only be a comfortable emotional state for so long. When anger begins to recede, bargaining takes over. Such thoughts as, *If I do better . . .*, or *Take this away and I promise to always . . .*, give us a sense of control within an uncontrollable situation. Anger and denial can cause us to lash out, but bargaining is usually internal. People can become stuck in the bargaining phase for too long, and might need to force themselves to talk about the deals they are trying to strike. When explored out loud with others, bargaining helps the bargainers understand what they can and cannot change in their new situation.

Stage 4. Depression

Once we acknowledge that our bargaining is in vain, a flood of sadness washes over us. This is where grief sinks in and begins to feel like a much heavier burden than ever before. We often withdraw from life and friends, unable to perform even simple tasks without feeling exhausted. Depression causes feelings such as, *What's the point? My life isn't worth living anymore*, or, *How can I continue on like this?* Many wounded warriors and their wives experience depression. This stage can feel endless and exhausting for both, but without it they will not be able to flush sadness out of their systems. Often without a period of depression—which allows the feelings of sorrow and hopelessness to come to a head— moving forward cannot continue.

Stage 5. Acceptance

When the dense fog of depression lifts, those dealing with grief will find themselves in a land of acceptance. However, acceptance is far from being "okay" or "fine" with a loss. Instead it is an acknowledgment of the truth of the situation, an adjustment to the "new" new. We might not be "fine" with it, but we accept it. A surge of inspiration often ascends from the rubble during this period, and we think thoughts such as, *This doesn't define me, I have a greater purpose*, and *I can help others through my adversity.*

When the wife of a wounded warrior reaches the acceptance stage, she might feel weary at first. But with acceptance comes the motivation to do the best she can with what she's got. Acceptance means making peace with what is, but it also leaves room for contemplating ways to making the situation even better.

It is important to note that these stages are not bound by a linear order. They can skip around randomly, popping up many times within the grief process. At a SPA Day, one wife shared the story of how she and her husband went through these stages at different times and at different paces, as they both grieved the loss of their former life.

She said, "I was sprinting for a couple months, but when the bargaining phase became a marathon, I couldn't keep passing the water stations. I had to stop, refresh myself, and reach out for help."

In addition to forcing us to recognize when we need help from others, these stages also offer growth in the forms of empathy, listening skills, patience, appreciation, a desire to spread awareness, and strengthening the bonds of friendship and family ties.

Denial, anger, depression, bargaining, and acceptance are more than stages; they are like the seasons of growth. A growing tree fluctuates between expansion and retraction—losing leaves in the fall, then blossoming in the spring—but every year it becomes stronger. Every person who makes it through the five stages comes out wiser, kinder, and more powerful than ever before. By understanding the universal pattern of these Five Stages of Grief *Growth*, we can foster patience with ourselves and others, and find the inner grace we need to guide ourselves toward healing.

* * *

The concept of PTG might seem counterintuitive. How can you grow and suffer at the same time?

PTG doesn't mean living with a total lack of suffering while wisdom builds. It means that real, important growth can—and often will—occur within the context of pain and loss. In fact, when it comes to wounded warriors, some measure of stress or pain might be necessary for significant growth to occur. Along with self-awareness and motivation, PTG might also foster resilience for future events that might otherwise become traumatic. This growth makes people who have lived through trauma more equipped to deal with trauma, which is pretty miraculous when you think about it.

It's also a testament to the deep-seated, stubborn, glorious strength of the human soul. We can come through the fire, burnt and smoking, but ready to start extinguishing every other fire we see. Not all wives of wounded warriors experience PTG, but the ones who do are like phoenixes rising from the ashes, using their pain to build their strength and tapping that strength to make their lives richer, fuller, and more rewarding than ever.

CHAPTER 8

WOUNDED WARRIOR WOMEN

I had my legs blown off in Iraq, and because I had my legs blown off in Iraq, people are listening to me. I'm not going to get my legs back, and that's fine, but if that gives me a platform to talk about the things that are important to me, like education and jobs, that's great.
—TAMMY DUCKWORTH, *U.S. Congresswoman*

WHEN YOU THINK of war, you think of men, right? Not so fast. Although male soldiers have dominated wars both past and present, women also have played integral roles in combat warfare throughout history. And we continue to play significant and sometimes controversial roles, both in making war and in keeping peace.

Hundreds of years ago, women warriors fought alongside men, assuming a wide range of ranks from foot soldier to high commander. Celtic warriors like Boudicca and Grace O'Malley, along with more well-known historic figures including Helen of

Troy, Joan of Arc, Lysistrata, and Cleopatra were all instrumental in planning and executing wars on behalf of their home nations. In their book *Hell Hath No Fury: True Stories of Women at War from Antiquity to Iraq*, authors Robin Cross and Rosalind Miles explore how women's presence in conflicts both large and small has influenced the tides of war. The book opens with a telling quote from the mayor of Montmartre, who witnessed women fighting in France's republican uprising of 1871, saying, "They fought like devils. Far better than the men."

But by the nineteenth century—when that rebellion took place—the presence of women warriors was the exception, not the rule. Hundreds of years earlier, the influence of patriarchy and the acceptability of misogyny had begun to grow, and women were forced out of the ranks and relegated to caretaker roles. Removing women from front-line positions was a clear and decisive way to strip us of power, a power that had previously been shared between genders. Whether expressed through religions like Judaism, Christianity, or Islam; through a social-military system like the Roman or Chinese Empire; or as a philosophy like Confucianism, the message to women everywhere was clear: your power is limited. In the Book of Timothy, St. Paul makes this plain, saying, "I permit no woman to usurp authority over a man."

The reversal of women's rights put the power firmly in the hands of men for many years. Women weren't permitted to plan or fight in wars for centuries and took a backseat while their male counterparts defended their nations. Only towards the end of the twentieth century have women such as Golda Meir, Condoleezza Rice, and Hillary Clinton regained their place in councils of war, reclaiming a right that their sisters enjoyed from the dawn of recorded time.

And today, with changes in military policy and shifts in thinking, the number of women taking part in modern-day battles is rising.

Approximately 14 percent of members of the U.S. military are women today, and more women are joining the armed forces all the time. The nature of combat in modern conflicts—the 360-degree battlefield—has meant that women, who couldn't take on combat roles until recently, are now able to step into combat positions. As you read this, somewhere a woman is cleaning her rifle, packing her ammunition, and preparing to go to battle.

Although these numbers indicate shifting gender norms, they also mean that more and more women are returning home wounded. And because gender equality is a work in progress, some of these women are not formally recognized as combat veterans. A few brave women have captured the spotlight, like Martha McSally, who flew A-10 ground attack missions in Afghanistan and became the first woman to command a United States Air Force combat squadron. Tammy Duckworth, whose story you'll read in this chapter, is also a recent military heroine, a person I have never met but would love to. Her story is highlighted in the media. Her journey truly inspires us on many levels.

When I first started offering SPA Day, I welcomed women warriors to join our discussions, too. Through the eight years that I've sponsored the event, only a handful of wounded women have attended, so, over time, the programming has become mainly for the partners of wounded warriors. The wounded women who do attend have told me that, although their spouses were very supportive, they never offered to give up their careers to care for their wounded wives. By keeping their careers going, these husbands maintained their positive self-esteem and didn't become resentful. The role reversal of a man as the caregiver is a huge adjustment, and in most cases not one that husbands are willing to make.

But caregiving is expected of women. During times when we were banned from the battlefield, women supported and cared for the men who returned from war broken and wounded. Women have gone to war as doctors and nurses, knowing that their innate caregiving skills and essential medical expertise could make a difference even away from the trenches and gunfire. Women like Florence Nightingale and Clara Barton were women of action, unafraid to enter dangerous territory so they could help and heal injured soldiers. Those caregiving and healing roles will always be essential.

But how might the modern-day warrior in each of us lead women in solving social problems? How can we follow in the footsteps of such legendary leaders as Helen of Troy, Joan of Arc, and Cleopatra?

We can stand up and speak out when we see injustice. We can encourage each other as we struggle to support our broken and ailing families. We can learn to use our feminine powers to heal the wounds of war. And we can take our place on the front lines to demonstrate our bravery and skill alongside our male counterparts.

After learning of the heroics that wives of wounded warriors undertake as tireless caregivers, I also began collecting stories of wounded women warriors, many of whom have returned home with a self-assigned mission to help their fellow veterans and citizens. Let's hear from a few of the women who have put themselves on the front lines of public policy and are changing how our government handles the flood of veterans and their families who desperately need help.

TAMMY: SAVING ONESELF, SAVING OTHERS

Have you ever gone through a stretch of overwhelming, stressful days and—when you finally came up for air—wondered where your week went?

Tammy Duckworth has experienced the nightmare version of this everyday phenomenon. She woke up from a dramatic week in 2004 with zero recollection of the previous eight days, and the realization that her right leg was gone up to her hip bone and her left leg had been removed below the knee. She soon found out that her broken arm was also in danger of being amputated if the proper blood supply could not be leveled.

It might seem bizarre to refer to a victim of such a tragedy as "one of the lucky ones," but Tammy will attest that she was indeed fortunate to have come away with these injuries after a rocket-propelled grenade decimated her helicopter's cockpit. After all, she came away alive.

But she soon discovered that life as a wounded warrior was a mixed blessing, and constantly challenging. First, there was frustration and the need to come to grips with how difficult everything would be moving forward. In those early days, every battle was taxing. Every new obstacle meant tears, angry outbursts, confusion, and dismay. When Tammy was anxiously waiting for her body to heal so she could begin rehabilitation, there would often be unexpected setbacks and situations where little (if anything) was within her control. Her limbs would swell suddenly and without warning. Previously undiscovered shrapnel would appear through her skin and require immediate removal.

"Every day included visits by new teams of doctors," Tammy explained, "and I was forced to decode their medical jargon on the fly and get used to their varied and ever-changing treatment styles."

It was a long, aggravating, painful, and overwhelming process that could have transformed her into a withdrawn, angry, sullen person. But the difference between those who make it through the tunnel and those who stay trapped in the darkness is how they choose to interpret their situations. Tammy chose optimism and strength, showing the world that it was possible to overcome adversity with grace and flexibility. Her positive perspective gave her the capacity to surmount almost every obstacle thrown her way. She refused to be a victim, and instead embraced life with eager, open arms of gratitude.

During her healing journey, dormant muscles were roused and Tammy could feel her body creating new boundaries. She decided early on that sustaining her injuries at thirty-six—instead of in her early twenties, as many soldiers do—allowed her to feel gratitude for the many years she had enjoyed the use of her legs. She recognized that she could have died, and was grateful for every day of her life. She channeled her appreciation into positive thinking about her future. In particular, she hoped to be able to fly for the Army again someday.

Tammy was also thankful for her husband Bryan, who was her number one motivator. When we're facing down immense adversity, we may desperately want someone to be real with us, and Bryan provided that authenticity for Tammy. He commonly peppered her physical therapy sessions with playful humor. His quip, "You aren't turning all white this time," always conjured a smile from Tammy.

But although her husband provided vital support, at the end of the day Tammy called the shots—on her attitude, her goals, the direction of her energy for the day, and how she would interact with anyone she encountered. She continued to make strides not only in her own recovery process, but in her professional life as well. She's collected a Purple Heart along with nine other service-related honors, has spoken at three Democratic National Conventions, and has completed a PhD in human services.

Having experienced firsthand the wounded vet's struggles to survive, heal, and rejoin society, Tammy has made it her life's work to improve the odds for her disabled comrades. She has committed herself to ensuring that those who survive war and return to American soil no longer endure the headaches of lackluster health care or nonexistent governmental support.

She knew that she wanted to make change from the top down, so she began to pursue public office. She served as the director of the Illinois Department of Veterans Affairs, where she implemented many first-in-the-nation programs to alleviate suffering from PTS, improve TBI screening, and reduce homelessness among veterans. She went on to become assistant secretary of public and intergovernmental affairs for the VA, where she headed the department's effort to end veteran homelessness and championed initiatives for female veterans. She also implemented innovative efforts, including creating the Office of Tribal Government Relations. And—nearly a decade after her injury—she was elected to Congress.

In 2013, Tammy joined the U.S. House of Representatives to represent Illinois, making her the first Asian-American woman elected to Congress in her state *and* the first disabled woman to serve in the House. She is primed and more determined than ever to educate the top tiers of our government about the issues surrounding veterans' care.

In Congress, Tammy is focused on growing our economy by advocating for small businesses, investing in infrastructure, and cutting government waste and fraud, in addition to her efforts to improve the lives of our veterans. Tammy serves on the House Armed Services and the House Oversight and Government Reform committees. In just a handful of years, this bona fide Wonder Woman has built an impressive and important political career. She's a groundbreaker and a firebrand, letting her inner warrior shine through in everything she does.

In a culture that encourages dissatisfaction, Tammy exudes integrity, honor, and fearlessness. Even as her Black Hawk helicopter spun out of control during the grenade attack, she scrambled to safely land it so she could save her crew. Even in life-threatening danger, her dedication and bravery rose above the chaos. Tammy shares her story to offer hope and inspiration not only to veterans, but to anyone facing adversity. Her fight to regain control of her body has much in common with any unexpected and drastic change in health, ability, or daily life. And against difficult odds in our country's government, she pursues what she knows our bravest citizens need.

OLIVIA: ALLOWING TRAGEDY TO SHAPE SUCCESS

When dealing with the fallout of battlefield injuries, we often focus on physical suffering. But there is an inner wound that can be just as crippling to daily life once it attacks its victim: guilt. More specifically, survivor's guilt. Survivor's guilt (or survivor's syndrome) occurs when a person believes they have unjustly survived a traumatic event while others did not. It is said that "guilt is to the soul what pain is to the body," and for Olivia—a compact Latina woman with a rich, deep voice and shoulder-length black hair—this adage resonated.

Olivia joined the Marines in 2006, a year out of high school, not quite ready for college and hoping she could put her love of computers and problem solving to work supporting her country. She made her way through a few positions before becoming an avionics technician, installing and repairing the electronic systems on helicopters and aircraft. It was a position she loved and excelled at, and her efficiency and good humor made her a favorite among the pilots.

Although she could have spent her time performing her duties on American bases, she wanted her skills to be of use to her fellow Marines and did two tours in Iraq. On her second tour, she was traveling with a convoy that included air support, and they were ambushed. Out of nowhere, grenades were being lobbed at the Humvees, and shots rang out in all directions. As Olivia crawled away from her decimated vehicle, both of her legs shredded by the explosion, she watched overhead as the gunfire took down the pilot of a helicopter—a pilot who had become one of Olivia's closest friends within the unit, a man who had served as her mentor from the moment she arrived in Iraq. They'd both grown up in the Midwest and had bonded over the frustrations of small-town living, forging a strong connection and an important friendship. As she watched the helicopter go down in flames, images of their time together—laughing and sharing memories—flashed before her eyes.

"Why him? Why not me?" she asked over and over, after her comrade's helicopter plunged to the ground. "He was married and had a daughter who he'll never get to see grow up. He had everything to live for. I didn't have those kinds of ties. It should have been me instead."

During a SPA Day lunch, she told me her story as her eyes brimmed with tears. "My comrades were killed in an ambush, and I walked away with only an amputated leg." In addition to her pilot friend, four other members of her unit died in the attack.

Every day, she dealt with self-judgment, blame, and an overwhelming sense of responsibility for the tragedy. She became her own emotional hostage. Soon, Olivia's survivor's guilt manifested as depression and rage.

"When I returned home, I withdrew from the world," she explained. "I didn't have a spouse to help me, and when friends and family reached out, I lashed out. I even considered hurting myself and felt like I was constantly trying to distract my anxious mind."

In the early stages of survivor's guilt, many people resist seeking support for their symptoms. They might feel they do not have the right to "complain" about their own situation, since they have it "easier" than others. And since they feel they have it "easier" than others, they assume they should automatically be more positive. When they can't muster any positivity, they feel even more guilt for their shortcomings. It's a harsh cycle of self-abuse.

During this time of silent desperation, though, Olivia discovered the Wounded Warrior Project, which helped her make sense of her past experiences, provided a bridge of connection with others, and served as a launchpad for her future hopes and ambitions. A specific program within the Wounded Warrior Project made all the difference for Olivia: Project Odyssey, which helps veterans overcome combat stress through outdoor, rehabilitative retreats that encourage a connection with nature and with their peers.

Through Project Odyssey, Olivia made a pivotal and lifesaving shift in her mind-set. She once again found the camaraderie of others who understood her plight, and that helped accelerate the healing process. She invited her friends and family to become involved with the Wounded Warrior Project so they could gain a deeper understanding of what she was going through, an invitation that proved vital to helping her relationships improve. Her sister—who had been confused and distant since Olivia's return home—found the program incredibly helpful. Learning about the impact of PTS on daily activities, and being forced to confront her own discomfort with Olivia's amputation, helped to shift her perspective and change her behaviors. After several heart-wrenching conversations during WWP gatherings, the two women reforged their bond and are now closer than ever.

Olivia did what everyone must do when faced with guilt that's holding them back: she felt it, expressed it, and found a space where she could process and release it.

She shares this wisdom with those facing the damaging effects of guilt in their lives: "It's so important to connect with other warriors and to share that same teamwork you had in the military. Individually, we're strong. Together, we're invincible."

Project Odyssey reignited Olivia's inner fire and got her mental wheels turning. After doing some more research, Olivia enrolled in the Wounded Warrior Project TRACK program in Jacksonville, Florida. The program helps wounded warriors transition from military to civilian life by offering guidance with career training and job placement. She was eager to put her computer skills back to work, but wasn't sure where or how to do it.

"Through the . . . TRACK program, I looked for work that would let me continue to help other injured warriors find their places in civilian life," she said.

Despite the personal and emotional advances she'd made outside the military, Olivia still felt that she'd found her purpose and calling in the Army. She wanted that feeling of belonging to become part of her life now that she was no longer in the military, but struggled to see how she could achieve this.

Olivia confessed, "What kept me up at night was not knowing what I was going to do. I still wanted to be with my platoon and figure out a way to do what I was doing before. The fact that my soldiers were still over there motivated me to find some way to continue being part of the fight."

Ever the tenacious trooper, Olivia set her sights on developing a way to fight on the front lines—for the troops—from her desk chair. And she found it through her experience with TRACK, which both built her confidence and revealed her inner entrepreneur. Instead of working for an established company, Olivia chose to become an independent IT contractor for the Warriors to Work program, a program with similar goals to TRACK. Warriors to Work provides career guidance and support services to WWP alumni interested in transitioning to the civilian workforce. In addition to helping warriors find new career paths, the program supports employers by connecting them with qualified candidates and providing information and education about combat-related injuries. Warriors to Work wants its participants to be in for the long haul, so trainers facilitate a productive onboarding process to help develop long-lasting relationships with both veterans looking for careers and employers looking to hire veterans. It was a perfect fit for Olivia, and she was so glad to have found her niche.

She was surprised to find, however, that being a woman in the IT field was more of a stumbling block back home than it had ever been overseas. Olivia was one of several independent contractors hired by Warriors to Work, and she ended up butting heads with some of the men she worked alongside.

"I didn't expect my gender to be a problem," she said, "and even when it clearly was a problem for others, I just kept my focus on the work. I figured I'd show them I could keep up—even do better than them—and eventually they'd lay off the girl jokes."

Her strategy worked. While several male contractors have been let go, Olivia's superior problem-solving skills and work ethic impressed the Warriors to Work team, and they've kept her on for several years. She now even has a small team to manage, and thrives on the added responsibility.

By partnering with this innovative program to leverage the vast experience and capabilities of veterans and wounded warriors, Olivia found a way to support the government she once physically fought for, without ever leaving her office. It was a savvy, soulful, and skillful move.

"Our veterans want to contribute and make a difference, and they have the leadership experience and technical skills to do that," she said. "I'm so glad I'm working for a company that helps them put their talents to work."

Olivia knows her wounds will never heal completely, and she is forever altered by her combat experience, but she has worked hard to ensure that the remaining survivor's guilt she feels is integrated into her whole self. Her story has become an honorable one. The disturbing symptoms of her lingering guilt have faded away and been replaced by wisdom, compassion, and a dedication to lifelong service.

Each day, Olivia's work for a program that helps wounded warriors find rewarding careers in the civilian workforce fuels her commitment to serve herself, her fellow veterans, and the country she will always be proud to uphold. It's hard not to admire Olivia's selfless drive and her truly American spirit. And as a fearless woman in a male-dominated field, she teaches us to worry less about fitting into glass slippers and more about shattering glass ceilings.

CHAPTER 9

THE HEALING POWER OF STORYTELLING: REASONS TO TELL YOUR STORY

*And sometimes remembering will lead to a story, which
makes it forever. That's what stories are for. Stories are
for joining the past to the future. Stories are for those
late hours in the night when you can't remember how
you got from where you were to where you are. Stories
are for eternity, when memory is erased, when there is
nothing to remember except the story.*

—TIM O'BRIEN, *The Things They Carried*

PICTURE THIS: YOU'RE sitting around a table with a
group of girlfriends, sipping coffee and chatting. One of the
women starts telling a story from her own life, and as you listen
to her strong words and passionate voice, you can tell she's
digging deep. Then she catches herself, looks embarrassed, and
apologizes for rambling, or self-centeredness, or monopolizing
the conversation.

Sound familiar?

Most women have either seen this happen or been that woman themselves, the one who allows herself to tell her story, then backs down quickly in fear and shame. I believe this pattern continues because the world would still prefer that women be seen and not heard. After all the strides we've made over the decades, some women still think we should be small, quiet, and totally selfless. Talking about ourselves too much is seen as conceit and self-involvement.

And that's because telling your story—sharing your struggles and triumphs with an audience that listens and cares—is one of the most powerful actions a person can take. Casting yourself as the hero in your own tale—seeing your journey on the larger stage of the world and recognizing your power to create change—helps cultivate empathy and perspective. And when you won't or can't tell your story, you can end up feeling trapped, alone, lost, and constantly wondering what's missing from your life.

If a wife attends SPA Day and shares her story with just one other person, that one witness might become a bridge to others. SPA Day is a welcoming, safe setting for telling stories that can foster the feeling of belonging to a tribe or family that will support the storyteller.

All women should feel empowered to tell their stories, but doing so is especially important to the wives of wounded warriors. Many recognize how important it is for a veteran to tell his story no matter how reluctant he might be to do so. But it's also essential that his wife tell her story, and that both feel they're being heard. Many wives withhold their stories, both because the stories are painful to tell and because they fear our closed-off culture won't hear and accept them. But if they don't tell these stories, they can't heal. Not fully.

I wish I could unite the entire community through these gatherings, but not all wives can attend SPA Day. Luckily, there are other ways to actively encourage storytelling and tap into its energy for yourself. Just as the women who attend SPA Day share their stories with listeners who become bridges to others, every person reading this book can take the stories they've read as permission to tell their own stories. In fact, I urge you to take it as an assignment to do so. Open up, be honest and vulnerable, and unleash your story without apology. We women need to step up and reclaim the healing power of storytelling for ourselves. Here are some more reasons why:

1. Telling your story keeps you healthy.

Every time you share your story with a caring, attentive listener, you release stress. As you spin your tale and explore it out loud with another person, the stress hormones cortisol and epinephrine ebb, and the healing chemicals oxytocin, dopamine, nitric oxide, and endorphins begin to flow. This amounts to giving your immune system an internal boost and can even help you feel better if you're sick. Telling your story helps your nervous system relax and can help heal your mind of depression, anxiety, fear, anger, and feelings of disconnection. Sometimes you don't know you are drowning when you are trying to be everyone else's anchor. As a caretaker, you need to adapt to the trauma so you don't become disabled yourself.

2. Opening up reminds you that you are not alone.

If I had to boil down everything I've learned from more than eight years of holding SPA Day, it would be this: no one is alone. So many of us are wrongly convinced that we're isolated, disconnected beings, wrestling with our suffering in a vacuum. But it's simply not true. And when you tell your story, you see that clear as day.

When you summon the bravery to share your story with others, you'll be amazed by how quickly kindred souls begin to appear in your life. You'll begin to feel as if you've found your tribe. Storytelling creates new communities, but it can also knit existing communities closer together. It becomes a verbal collective history that transforms storytellers and listeners alike into communal witnesses.

3. Sharing your past lights the path to your future.

If you want to build a new cell phone, you'd better know how the old one works. Similarly, if you want to build a better you, you have to go back and know how you worked in the past. When you share the story of your personal journey, you give yourself the chance to examine your past decisions, mistakes, and triumphs so you can be wiser and stronger as you move into the future. Doing this forces you to contemplate essential questions:

- What were your strengths and weaknesses?
- What do you need to change to build a better you?
- What did you do right and do you want to continue doing?

4. Stories foster authentic connections.

Do you know that when you tell your story without holding back—bravely sharing details and emotions that might seem "too personal" on the surface—you have the chance to create an authentic connection with someone else? If you water down or sugarcoat your story, you'll miss that connection. Every time you show your true colors and find another person who loves and accepts you despite your mistakes and flaws, you grow stronger. But that kind of support and validation can only come with true vulnerability.

TIPS ON GETTING STARTED

Do you feel ready to open up, be honest and vulnerable, and unleash your story without apology?

Even if you're hesitating, try to push outside your comfort zone. Find a way to tell your story now. And not just for use in single discussion, but daily or weekly or at least once per month. What is really going on for you? Telling your story will help you discover answers to questions you didn't even know you had.

- Might you share one of the stories in this book and say how it has affected you? Which parts of yourself come alive as you share your feelings and thoughts?
- Brainstorm a list of people you might talk to. Why do you think those specific people come to mind?
- When would you be able to talk to at least one of those people?
- Where do you picture yourself talking to that person, and which story do you imagine telling them?

It is essential that each of us find a way to share the experiences and events that weigh down our consciousness. We need to muster up the bravery to tell our friends and families, "I have to share this with you, or it might just drag me down." We need to acknowledge that when we make our stories known, we increase our personal power exponentially.

The women who have shared their stories in this book have said over and over again how vital it was for them to bring their experiences and emotions to light. I hope you will take their example to heart and shine a light on your own story. Doing so will undoubtedly change your life for the better.

Epilogue

I hate war as only a soldier who lived it can, as one who has seen the futility, its stupidity.
                              —DWIGHT D. EISENHOWER

SPA DAYS ARE held now in San Diego, Los Angeles, and throughout the U.S. It's my hope to continue expanding the program until it's accessible to the wives of wounded warriors all across our country. They deserve the respite of a quiet day's relaxation and the chance to connect with others who understand their lives and struggles on a personal level. I want this program to grow until it touches more lives than can be counted, helps more women than it leaves behind.

But it's not just the wives who benefit from SPA Day. I too am growing and learning from the women for whom I advocate. By providing them with a day of support, purpose, and appreciation, I access an inspiring community of amazing people. I'm overwhelmed by the gratitude that SPA Day attendees express, and I do my best to let them know that gratitude flows both ways.

I initially named my foundation Mother Lover Fighter Sage after the inner dimensions of women, archetypes that arise from our collective unconscious. They are, essentially, the various shades that contribute to the overall colors of our personas. I've studied the way these four specific archetypes recur in women throughout history and have experienced firsthand how they can balance us. I've also witnessed them as forces that influence society and observed that understanding them on an individual level helps foster phenomenal personal growth.

On these pages, we've watched women explore each of these archetypes in transformative ways. We've seen these women as Mothers—not only to their biological children, but to the men they've married, expressing their nurturing personalities through selfless caregiving.

We've seen them as both the dedicated and the obscured Lover. They've proclaimed their undying and unquenchable loves for their wounded husbands, but at times they've also buried their passions and repressed their sexual energy.

We've seen them charge into battle for themselves, for their children, and for their beloved spouses. These women may never leave American soil, but they are warriors and Fighters in their own right. They fight fiercely for the care their loved ones deserve, for balance within their families, and for the recovery of some sense of normality. But perhaps the hardest battle they will face is within themselves.

Imagine how quickly warriors must adapt when they enter their first battle. Up until that moment, it has all been training and theory. But at the crucial moment, their survival instincts kick in, partner up with skills acquired in training, and equip them to deal with their first "real-time" encounter.

The women featured in this book experience something similar when they find themselves on the other side of the "for better or for worse" vow. That is the battleground. That is when they find out what they're really made of, and their commitment, character, and courage rise up and take over. There isn't a sanctioned holiday or even a patriotic song for these women, but they fight anyway. Perhaps that is the most quintessentially Fighter-like trait they possess: the ability to carry on when others might quit, because their very natures tell them they *must* keep going.

Luckily, we've also seen them downshift from battle mode to process their experiences, to learn, grow, and strive to share their hard-won wisdom with others. The Sage archetype closes the circle: the wisdom and insight these women offer to those they nurture *does* come back to them during their own times of need. The Sage within each of us will always see and reach out to the Sage within others. In sharing their inspiring stories and the lessons they've learned, these wise women have taught me to listen to my own inner wisdom.

Fully realizing all of our archetypical dimensions as we move through life's journey—by acknowledging and exercising all of these inner guides—truly sets us free. The women we've met on these pages are reaching for that hard-won freedom with all their might, and their fearlessness can inspire us all.

My hope for the brave wounded warriors and their spouses is simple: may they continue to find their strengths and learn from them.

My dream for us all is that we find the compassion and means to help and support wounded warriors and their spouses. Let us strive to help them rebuild their lives in the aftermath of two horrendous and ongoing wars, from which even more wounded warriors and their wives will continue to emerge. By helping them, we help ourselves become more compassionate, more aware, and more connected to our fellow human beings.

My dream for the world is an end to war, and although I know that dream seems far out of reach right now, I believe it's a dream worth having. If I've learned anything from the amazing women who have shared their stories, journeys, and insights with me, it is this: love heals. And perhaps with enough understanding, support, and love, we can heal the world.

Acknowledgments

A WORK OF this magnitude cannot be completed without the help of others.

I want to first express my gratitude and respect to all the wives of wounded warriors who have entrusted me with their stories and their healing journeys.

I also want to thank, with all my heart, the others who contributed to this important project:

Larry Edwards and Sally McGraw, my editors, who believed in and labored over this book with exceeding skill and devotion. They share with me the hope that, with it, we can make a significant contribution to healing and peacemaking in our troubled world.

Lorie Van Tilburg, who helped me grow the SPA Day program so that we could reach women all over the United States.

Farrell Gallagher, LCSW, MFT, for his contribution as a clinical consultant.

My daughters Jacqui and Christine for their editorial support and website design.

Finally, a big thank you to the good folks at Köehler Books for their faith and support throughout this process. From the beginning, the press appreciated the importance of a book that would capture the emotions and voices of the women behind the wounded warriors.

APPENDICES

APPENDICES

Appendix I

SUGGESTED QUESTIONS FOR BOOK DISCUSSIONS

CHAPTER 1: WHY IS MY HUSBAND SO ANGRY?

1. What are the symptoms of PTS that you see in yourself or your mate?
2. Do you or your loved one experience night terrors or daytime flashbacks related to a specific crisis or trauma that occurred more than six months ago?
3. Have you found escape in excessive use of drugs, alcohol, food, or pornography since this event to find temporary relief?
4. Are you more depressed, sullen, or isolated than before the traumatic event?
5. Are you more easily startled, or do you react with anger, rage, or fear to something that might not have bothered you much before your trauma?
6. In speaking with counselors at the Wounded Warrior Battalion in San Diego and Camp Pendleton, I learned that most would prefer that posttraumatic stress be called an injury, not

a disorder. That's why I dropped the D at the end of the abbreviation for the purposes of this book, using PTS instead of PTSD. Some sufferers treat PTS like back pain—there are different treatments to prevent the symptoms from recurring, and if you don't discuss your situation with others and explore your options, the perfect treatment for your specific situation might remain undiscovered. What have you found that helps control the symptoms of PTS in *your* life?

7. If you have another medical diagnosis such as attention deficit disorder or bipolar disorder, are you comfortable being out in the open with it? What are the measures you take to control it? If you view yourself (or your warrior loved one) as having a professionally diagnosed disorder rather than as someone experiencing expected reactions from combat, does it affect your feelings and thoughts about yourself (or your loved one)?

8. Does being out in nature or enjoying outdoor activities, like fishing or skiing, help your state of mind? What other activity-related resources have you found?

9. Some of the wives say attending church helps them cope. Has your church, temple, mosque, or other religious organization helped you? What other support system have you found in times of crisis?

10. If you have used drugs, alcohol, food, or pornography to escape, what are your feelings about the usefulness of each method and its shortcomings? How might you seek help in replacing detrimental remedies with healing remedies?

CHAPTER 2: TRAUMATIC BRAIN INJURY

1. If you or your spouse lives with a TBI, was it something you knew about right away? If not, what made you suspect something might be wrong other than visible injuries?
2. How did this injury impact your family's life at first? How does it impact your life now? What has changed? What are the factors that created this change?
3. What activity or routine did you formerly enjoy that you were forced to change when TBI entered your life? How do you feel about that loss?
4. Who became your support system? Who understood your situation, and who didn't?

CHAPTER 3: LIVING WITH IRON MAN

1. Did you recognize the Amputee Coalition of America's six phases of recovery as stages that you or your spouse experienced? Which phase was the longest or hardest for your family?
2. Were you involved in the decision to amputate a limb? What do you remember about that experience? Is there anything you would have done differently, knowing what you know now?
3. Has your wounded warrior experienced phantom pain? How does he or she manage it?
4. If you've supported your spouse through multiple surgeries, are you familiar with the "boomerang effect" that can be part of the recovery process?
5. What's your best tool for dealing with people who stare or who lack understanding about amputees and amputation?

6. The amputees in this chapter returned to the activities they loved—sports and playing music—after long rehabilitation periods. What activity would you or your partner most like to regain? What steps are you taking to make that possible?

CHAPTER 4: A REASON TO LIVE

1. How has suicide touched your life? When did this happen, and how did it affect you?
2. Can you identify the signs and indicators of suicide risk in a family member or friend? What are they?
3. How can you make yourself aware of the phone numbers for available resources in case of an emergency? Where can you post them? What might you add to 911 and the numbers for crisis hotlines?
4. Veterans often contemplate suicide because, back at home and injured, they feel purposeless and impotent. Have you seen this in your wounded warrior or felt it yourself? How do you help combat those dark feelings?
5. There is a strong link between PTS and suicide attempts. What resources could help you cope more effectively with your own or your partner's PTS so you avoid hitting bottom?
6. Career goals, travel, and sports—activities that provide a sense of accomplishment—are often vital in the aftermath of a suicide attempt. They can also help prevent an attempt in the first place. What goals has your wounded warrior set that you can help him or her work toward? What are the goals you have set for yourself?

CHAPTER 5: SEXUALITY

1. Is sex important to your marriage? Is it just the icing on the cake, or would your relationship feel hollow without it?
2. How has your sex life changed? What's worse? What's better?
3. When was the last time you brought a new technique, position, or toy into the bedroom? Could doing so help your intimacy?
4. In this chapter, many wives shared workarounds they were using to get through sexual dry spells. Have you tried any of them? Celibacy? Pleasuring yourself? Stepping outside the marriage? What worked best?
5. Have you dealt with a link between sexual and aggressive energy? Did you find a way to make it work for you as a couple?
6. If you or your spouse has suffered from a genital wound, what was the hardest part of recovery for you both? What was the most surprising part of recovery?
7. Some say the primary sex organ is the mind. Can you get beyond changes in physical form and connect with your partner psychologically, emotionally, and spiritually?

CHAPTER 6: STAY OR GO?

1. Have you considered leaving your marriage? What stopped you? What would be your breaking point?
2. What would be the hardest part of leaving for you? For your spouse? For your children?
3. What would be easier for you if you left?

4. What self-care practices are you establishing for yourself? If self-care has fallen by the wayside, what can you begin doing now that will help restore your energy?

5. Amy and Mary, the wives who shared their stories in this chapter, both left their marriages. How did reading their stories affect you? Did you find yourself judging them? Envious of them?

6. Do you realize you always have options, even if they're not desirable?

7. Do you give yourself permission to consciously consider the choices you have, given your circumstances?

8. Is it acceptable for you to think in terms of what's best for *you*?

CHAPTER 7: NOT JUST SURVIVING BUT THRIVING

1. Have you or anyone you know experienced posttraumatic growth (PTG)? How did it manifest?

2. PTG can be big or small. Do you find yourself advocating more, or asking more questions? This is PTG. Are you able to appreciate the small pleasures in life? Also PTG. Having read this chapter, what new feelings or behaviors can you now identify as part of your own growth process? Have you or your spouse dealt with survivor's guilt? Did talking about it help? If not, what actions helped to lessen the guilt?

3. Can you relate to Jenny's "silver lining sightings"? Which have appeared in your own life? Are there any you can actively pursue for yourself and your family?

4. Have you witnessed the five stages of grief growth? How did they change you? Which stage was the hardest? Which helped you the most in your journey to healing?

CHAPTER 8: WOUNDED WARRIOR WOMEN

1. If you're a wounded woman warrior, did your husband or partner offer to give up his career to care for you? If not, why not?
2. How do you feel about women in combat?
3. How did reading Tammy's story make you feel? Could you ever advocate for veterans' rights outside of your own family? Are there small steps you can take to help the veteran community?
4. Are you aware of companies or organizations near you that actively seek veterans as potential employees?
5. Do you know of other programs that help combat-injured veterans transition to civilian work?
6. Have you experienced bias in the workplace like Olivia?

Appendix II

RESOURCES

ONE OF THE most wonderful surprises of sponsoring SPA Day was meeting other women who had started foundations to help wounded warriors and their wives. In 2014, I attended a fundraiser for Operation Family Caregiver and the Southern Caregiver Resource Center to hear Katy, a SPA Day attendee and wife of a wounded warrior, speak. There I met Lorie Van Tilburg, the resource center's executive director. I immediately asked Lorie to speak at our sixteenth SPA Day.

Lorie was inspirational, uplifting, and helpful. Soon after that, the Southern Caregiver Resource Center and the Rosalynn Carter Institute for Caregiving came on board to cosponsor SPA Day and help it grow. Lorie introduced me to Laura J. Bauer, national program director for Operation Family Caregiver, who had these words:

> Most of these family members, neighbors, and friends do not call themselves "caregivers," but they are the vital system that supports those suffering from seen and unseen injuries on a daily basis. Their unselfish

contributions often come at great cost to their own mental health and well-being.

Because these hidden heroes often do not recognize that they will also be caregivers—in addition to any other role they currently occupy (wife, parent, battle buddy)—they may not seek out and learn about the free, confidential, and effective support that is available to assist them in this new role.

The stories in this book mention many wonderful programs that can help, and the list of resources includes others as well. There are many support groups, such as those offered by Operation Homefront, caregiver retreats offered by Hearts of Valor, online communities such as the Military and Veteran Caregiver Network, the Rosalynn Carter Institute's evidence-based, tailored, face-to-face Operation Family Caregiver program, and more. Hope and help come in many forms.

But, sadly, military caregiver support programs are underutilized by the very population they were developed to help. Unlike the *Field of Dreams* premise of "build it and they will come," these caregivers either don't know about the programs in the first place, don't think they qualify for them, or are still stuck in the self-defeating mind-set of thinking they can do it all without any help.

So, what can you do? Talk to your friends, colleagues, and family members who are supporting a service member or veteran, and let them know that the things they do for their beloved vets indeed qualify them as "caregivers." Tell them about the programs listed here that are available to assist them in this new role. Reinforce the truth that the healthiest way to care for another is to care for yourself first. Remind these hidden heroes that reaching out for help is a sign of strength.

VETERAN AND GOVERNMENTAL SERVICE ORGANIZATIONS

Directory of Veterans Service Organizations—published as an informational service by the Office of the Secretary of Veterans Affairs. www.va.gov/vso/

FOCUS (Families OverComing Under Stress): Family Resilience Training for Military Families—teaches practical skills to help families overcome common challenges related to a parent's military service, to communicate and solve problems effectively, and to successfully set goals together. focusproject.org

Military Order of the Purple Heart—chartered by Congress in 1958 and composed of military men and women who have received the Purple Heart medal for wounds suffered in combat, the organization's membership supports all veterans and their families with nationwide programs. www.purpleheart.org

National Suicide Prevention Lifeline—operated by the Substance Abuse and Mental Health Services Administration, an agency within the U.S. Department of Health and Human Services, the lifeline offers 1-800-273-TALK (8255), a 24-hour, toll-free, confidential suicide-prevention hotline available to anyone in suicidal crisis or emotional distress. www.suicidepreventionlifeline.org

The Purple Heart Foundation—serves as the fundraising arm of the Military Order of the Purple Heart for providing support to veterans and their families through grants, outreach programs, and donations to organizations whose programs help veterans. www.purpleheartfoundation.org

U.S. Department of Veterans Affairs (VA)—provides benefits and services to veterans. www.va.gov

VA Caregiver Support—has several support and service options available both in and out of the home to help veterans and their caregivers. www.caregiver.va.gov

Veterans Health Administration—integrates a health-care system consisting of 150 medical centers and nearly 1,400 community-based outpatient clinics, community living centers, Vet Centers, and domiciliary programs. www.va.gov/health/

Veterans of Foreign Wars—an instrumental voice in establishing services for veterans and improving conditions at VA medical centers. www.vfw.org

VFW Assistance—offers a wide range of assistance programs aimed at helping veterans of every generation, including free, professional help filing or appealing a VA claim, scholarships for postsecondary education, and emergency financial relief when times get tough. www.vfw.org/Assistance/

Wounded Warrior Regiment—upholds the charge from the Commandant of the Marine Corps to provide longitudinal care and support for wounded, ill, and injured Marines and their families. www.woundedwarriorregiment.org

CAREGIVING RESOURCES

Administration for Community Living: Caregivers and Families (U.S. Department of Health and Human Services)—provides assistance to caregivers of older adults and people with disabilities, defining a caregiver as anyone who provides help to another person in need. www.acl .gov/Get_Help/Help_Caregivers/

California Caregiver Resource Centers—California's eleven nonprofit Caregiver Resource Centers serve more than 14,000 families and caregivers of adults affected by chronic and debilitating health conditions, including dementia; Alzheimer's disease; cerebrovascular diseases (such as stroke or aneurysms); degenerative diseases such as Parkinson's, Huntington's, and multiple sclerosis; or traumatic brain injury, among many others. www .caregiver.org/californias-caregiver-resource-centers

Caregiving Across the States: 50 State Profiles—www.caregiver .org/caregiving-across-states-50-state-profiles-2014

Elizabeth Dole Foundation – Uplifting military families and caregivers by strengthening the services afforded to them through innovation, evidence-based research, and collaboration. www.elizabethdolefoundation.org

Family Caregiver Alliance (National Center on Caregiving)—addresses the needs of families and friends providing long-term care for loved ones at home. Supported by the National Family Caregiver Support Program, aged/ disabled Medicaid waivers, and state-funded programs. www.caregiver.org

Military and Veteran Caregiver Network—offers peer-based support and services to connect caregivers with others who are giving care to members of the military or to veterans who are living with wounds, illness, or injury. milvetcaregivernetwork.org

Office on Women's Health: Caregiving (U.S. Department of Health and Human Services)—provides information on caregiving and where to obtain assistance and services. www.womenshealth.gov/aging/caregiving/

Operation Family Caregiver (OFC)—helps families of returning service members and veterans adjust to the "new normal" by coping more effectively with problems they never imagined related to post-traumatic stress, a TBI or a physical disability. OFC is a personalized, evidence-based problem-solving program tailored specifically to the struggles of each family. OFC Coaches teach families the skills needed to best navigate their challenges, resulting in stronger and healthier families. OFC is a program of the Rosalynn Carter Institute for Caregiving, begun with catalytic funding from Johnson & Johnson, and is available to families of all war eras. www.operationfamilycaregiver.org

Rosalynn Carter Institute for Caregiving—establishes local, state, and national partnerships committed to building quality, long-term home- and community-based services. www.rosalynncarter.org

Southern Caregiver Resource Center: Provides service for San Diego residents caring for an injured adult. caregivercenter .org

USC Center for Innovation and Research on Veterans & Military Families—aims to strengthen the transition of veterans and their families into the community through education, training, research, and partnerships. cir.usc.edu

U.S. Department of Health and Human Services—provides health services and fosters advances in medicine, public health, and social services. www.hhs.gov

NONPROFIT SERVICE ORGANIZATIONS

Easter Seals Military and Veterans Caregiver Training—
provides comprehensive training developed by Easter
Seals in collaboration with VA clinical experts to family
caregivers of eligible post-9/11 veterans as authorized by
the Caregivers and Veterans Omnibus Health Services Act
of 2010. www.easterseals.com/our-programs/military-
veterans/veterans-caregiver-training.html

Hearts of Valor (formerly known as Wounded Warrior Wives)—
offers retreats designed to help caregivers learn financial
preparedness, the logistics of managing a home, and
ways to handle the impact on relationships of trauma,
posttraumatic stress, traumatic brain injury, and
compassion fatigue. www.heartsofvalor.org

NAMI Homefront—offers a free, six-session educational
program for families, caregivers, and friends of military
service members and vets with mental health conditions.
www.nami.org/Find-Support/NAMI-Programs/NAMI
-Homefront

Patriots and Paws—provides veterans, active military, reservists,
and their families throughout Southern California with
basic home furnishings for newly acquired residences.
www.patriotsandpaws.org

Project Odyssey—helps veterans overcome combat stress
through outdoor, rehabilitative retreats. www
.woundedwarriorproject.org/programs/combat-stress
-recovery-program/project-odyssey.aspx

PsychArmor Institute – bridges the civilian-military divide
through free online education and a support center staffed
with mental health experts. A better understanding of
military culture and the veteran community can alleviate

challenges veterans and service members face when returning from war or transitioning into civilian life. www .psycharmor.org

SPA Day for Wives of Wounded Warriors—created by author Barbara McNally, founder of the Barbara McNally Foundation, SPA Day provides an opportunity for military wives who have been supporting their husbands to have a day for themselves to restore and rejuvenate at the Hotel del Coronado and other sites around the U.S., where they are pampered and enjoy the fellowship of other wives struggling with the same challenges. BarbaraMcNally.com

Warriors to Work—provides career guidance and support services to Wounded Warrior Project alumni interested in transitioning to the civilian workforce. www.woundedwarriorproject.org/programs/warriors-to -work.aspx

Wounded Warrior Project—helps injured service members aid and assist one another while providing unique, direct programs and services to meet their needs. www.woundedwarriorproject.org

THERAPEUTIC SERVICES

Note: These listings are not endorsements by the author. They were mentioned by contributors to this work and are listed here as examples of the many types of therapeutic services that offer assistance to veterans and their families. Many of the programs provide outdoor, recreational, and equine-assisted (horse) programs. Some of them are free or subsidized by charitable organizations to reduce the costs. More of these services can be found by searching online.

Classic Equestrian Assisted Family Services—offers military families an equine-assisted therapeutic program to help with the management of complex medical conditions; based in Dublin, Georgia. www.eagala.org/node/17408

EAGALA Military Services – global referral list of military-experienced EAGALA Certified professionals providing equine-assisted psychotherapy and personal development, www.eagala.org/military

Horses for Heroes—cowboy up, veterans, posttraumatic stress disorder, moral injury, active duty. www.horsesforheroes .com

Invictus Games—the Invictus games are an international multisport event in which wounded, injured, or sick armed-services personnel and their associated veterans take part in sporting events. www.invictusgamesfoundation.org

National Ability Center—offers a program to build self-esteem, confidence, and lifelong skills through sport, recreation, and educational programs; based in Park City, Utah. www .discovernac.org

Project Healing Waters—offers physical and emotional rehabilitation to disabled active military service personnel and veterans through fly-fishing and associated activities, including education and outings; based in La Plata, Maryland. www.projecthealingwaters.org

Ride 2 Recovery—offers cycling-based rehabilitation programs for veterans; based in Calabasas, California. ride2recovery .com

Vail Veterans Program—aims to transform injured veterans and their families through individualized outdoor recreation programs, building confidence and creating lifelong relationships; based in Vail, Colorado. www .vailveteransprogram.org

Warriors & Quiet Waters—employs the therapy of fly-fishing to heal traumatically wounded warriors; based in southwest Montana. warriorsandquietwaters.org

Wave Academy—provides aquatic therapy for veterans and caregivers; based in San Diego, California. waveacademy .org

Warrior Games—a multisport event for wounded, injured, or ill service personnel and veterans organized by the USDOD. warriorgames.dodlive.mil

Wounded Warrior Amputee Softball Team (WWAST)— to inspire and educate others while enhancing the health and welfare of wounded amputees through softball teams and camps. woundedwarrioramputeesoftballteam.org

Wounded Warrior Outdoors—offers therapeutic activities such as backpacking, fishing, hunting, trail expeditions, and social interactions for active-duty warriors in transition; based in Winter Garden, Florida. www.woundedwarrioroutdoors.com

References

Bilmes, Linda J. "The Financial Legacy of Iraq and Afghanistan: How Wartime Spending Decisions Will Constrain Future National Security Budgets." Harvard University, Kennedy School of Government Faculty Research, Working Paper Series RWP13-006, March 2013.

Carter, Rosalynn. *Helping Yourself Help Others: A Book for Caregivers.* New York City: Times Books, 1994. www.rosalynncarter.org

Edwards, Larry M. *Dare I Call It Murder? A Memoir of Violent Loss.* San Diego: Wigeon Publishing, 2013. www.dareicallitmurder.com

Frankl, Viktor E. *Man's Search for Meaning.* Boston: Beacon Press, 1998.

Kang, Han K., et al. "Suicide Risk among 1.3 Million Veterans Who Were on Active Duty during the Iraq and Afghanistan Wars." *Annals of Epidemiology* 25, no. 2 (February 2015): 96–100.

Kastle, Seth. *Why Is Dad So Mad?* Hays, KS: Tall Tale Press, 2015. www.kastlebooks.com

Kemp, Janet, and Robert Bossarte. "Suicide Data Report, 2012." U.S. Department of Veterans Affairs, Mental Health Services, Suicide Prevention Program. www.va.gov/opa /docs/suicide-data-report-2012-final.pdf

LaPlante, Matthew D. "Military Divorce on Rise." *The Salt Lake Tribune*, December 23, 2007.

Miles, Rosalind, and Robin Cross. *Hell Hath No Fury: True Stories of Women at War from Antiquity to Iraq.* New York City: Broadway Books, 2008.

O'Brien, Tim. *The Things They Carried.* New York City: Broadway Books, 1998.

Ramchand, Rajeev, et al. "Hidden Heroes: America's Military Caregivers." The RAND Corporation, April 2014. www .rand.org/pubs/research_reports/RR499.html

Solnit, Rebecca. *The Faraway Nearby.* New York City: Penguin Books, 2014. www.rebeccasolnit.net

Wood, David. "Beyond the Battlefield: From a Decade of War, an Endless Struggle for the Severely Wounded." *The Huffington Post*, April 16, 2012. www.huffingtonpost .com/2011/10/10/beyond-the-battlefield-part-1-tyler -southern_n_999329.html

Zoroya, Gregg. "Military Divorce Rate at Highest Level Since 1999." *USA Today*, December 13, 2011.

CPSIA information can be obtained
at www.ICGtesting.com
Printed in the USA
LVOW13s1617010317

525811LV00010B/970/P